THE TAO OF TREES

Poems that Reconnect you to
the Natural World and your Sacred Self

Maria Mar

Pachamama Collection
Words that connect you to the natural and sacred world

Copyright © 2018 by Maria Mar

All rights reserved. This book is protected by international copyright law. No part of this publication may be reproduced, distributed, appropriated, sold or transmitted in any form or by any means, including photocopying, recording, scanning or other electronic or mechanical methods, without the prior written permission of the publisher, except in the case of brief quotations embodied in critical reviews and certain other noncommercial uses permitted by copyright law. For permission requests, write to the publisher, addressed "Attention: Permissions," at the address below.

ShamansDance Publishing & Productions at
shamansdancepublishing@gmail.com

Ordering Information: Bulk rates and special activities are available on quantity purchases by corporations, associations, book clubs and others. For details, contact the publisher at the email above. See more in the back pages.

Printed in the United States of America
Cover design and art by: Maria Mar

ISBN
13 digit: 978-0-9843670-3-0
10 digit: 0-9843670-3-9

Book Categories: Poetry | Spirituality | Art | Self-help: self-healing | Nature: trees

First Edition

The Tao of Trees

Poems that Reconnect you to the Natural World and your Sacred Self

Poems and illustrations by

Maria Mar

ShamansDance Publishing & Productions, New York, 2018

Dedication

I dedicate this book to:

The Poet-trees who healed me. Thank you.

My friend Myrna Nieves who
first encouraged me to publish these poems
with their illustrations and
whose cultural leadership has nurtured
generations of Puerto Rican writers
and empowered Puerto Rican
women writers.

Every person, organization and movement helping save trees.

Teachers, parents and educators all over the world
who are doing their part to instill in our children
a love, respect and responsibility towards trees and nature.

Those who are working bravely to create a world
where humanity honors nature; including those
working to generate alternative sources of energy,
to help pick up plastic from the oceans,
to stop fracking and to reduce our carbon footprints.
Bless you all.

To tree lovers all over the world. Hug a tree today!

Table of Contents

Introduction: Healing with the Poet-trees   Page 11

Path of Beauty   Page 19
1. Poetry   Page 20
2. Beauty   Page 22
3. Celebration   Page 24
4. Awakening   Page 26
5. I have not yet heard a bird   Page 28

Path of The Heart   Page 31
6. Intimacy   Page 32
7. Love   Page 34
8. Joy   Page 36
9. Dancing   Page 38
10. The Wounded Healer   Page 40

Path of Co-creation   Page 43
11. Trust   Page 44
12. Growth   Page 46
13. Reciprocity   Page 48
Visual Poem: Trees Are   Page 51
14. Receptivity   Page 52
15. The Passage   Page 54

Path of Transformation   Page 57
16. Attention   Page 58
17. Seeing   Page 60
18. Opportunity   Page 62
19. Persistence   Page 64
20. Commitment   Page 66

Path of Presence   Page 69
21. Presence   Page 70
22. Oneness   Page 74
23. Now   Page 76
24. Power   Page 78
Oracle Art: The Tree of Life and Death   Page 83
25. The Trees are Smiling   Page 84

Path of Freedom   Page 89
26. Shapeshifting   Page 90
27. Non-attachment   Page 92
28. The Invitation   Page 94
Visual Poem: Poet-tree   Page 97
29. Passion   Page 98
30. Soul   Page 102

Path of Healing   Page 107
31. Meeting Pain   Page 108
32. Cleansing   Page 110
Visual Poem: I am Storm   Page 113
33. A Higher Dance   Page 116
34. The Messenger of Hope   Page 118

Resource Section   Page 121
Tree Love Campaigns   Page 122
Tao of Trees Audio Meditations   Page 124
Tao of Trees Life Reading   Page 125
Tao of Trees Portfolio   Page 126
Tao of Trees Live Poetry Journey *(For Presenters)*   Page 127
Bulk Orders   Page 138
Save the Trees Resources   Page 129
Raise Funds and Spread Tree Love *(For Organizations)*   Page 131

About Section   Page 133
About Maria Mar   Page 134
Where is Maria Mar?   Page 139
Request Maria Mar for your Event   Page 140
Other Books by Maria Mar   Page 141
More Poetry by Maria Mar   Page 151
Your Tree Love Pledge   Page 152

Introduction:

Healing with the Poet-trees

It was a winter of despair. I had lost all I had. Exhausted and sick, I sat looking through a window at the trees in a grove. As I connected to the trees my mind became empty. Sky Mind. I entered a profound silence and in that stillness the Poet-trees whispered healing poems from their magical hearts to my recovering soul.

Until that day I did not know that trees were poets. I loved trees and knew that they helped to center me in the truth of my soul, to ground my energies and connect to Earth Mother and to enter peace. But until that unforgettable moment, they had not whispered their verses into my heart.

Perhaps I had not been quiet enough or had not listen deep enough. But now trees revealed their voices to me.

Trees are Life

Our soul knows what we often forget: trees are at the center of the dance of life and death. They hold our lives in their hands. Trees hold Earth together, feed her creatures and give us the *Breath of life*. From the oxygen we breathe to the food we eat, our one legged siblings are at the center of our existence.

But we forget. We take trees for granted, like we do the air we breathe and the earth we walk. We are so busy doing and worrying that we no longer recognize their essential gifts. Few people slow down long enough to appreciate the trees that stand, like old sentinels, guarding our daily walk.

I remember a boy in my old Lower East Side neighborhood. He was hitting a tree with a bat. He was taking his anger out on the tree. I told him not to hit the tree.

"Why not?" he challenged. "It does not feel anything!"

"How do you know?" I asked. "Trees are living, breathing beings."

"They are?" the boy asked in shock. He dropped the bat and ran.

Had no one told him that trees and plants were living beings? Or had it been a science lesson that he did not connect to his own environment?

This memory stands in my mind as a metaphor of our relationship to trees in particular and to nature in general.

As a result of our separation from the natural world, we are destroying the trees and the habitats that sustain them without stopping to think that we are destroying ourselves.

Trees are Teachers and Communicators

Few of us stop to consider that the teachings, stories and knowledge of the past centuries have traveled in the skin of trees, for trees have been the source of papers and books for as long as humans have written.

This is not a coincidence, for trees are powerful teachers. Not only have they carried our memories, words and dreams on their backs; trees have memories of their own. These memories contain the memories of life itself. Even the rings inside trees tell the story of our solar system.

Trees have words of their own. These words come out of their own existence, their own body, their stillness and their love; for in their quiet generosity trees give more than food, air or shade.

Trees taught me the *Art of Giving and Receiving*. They modeled true leadership to me. When I lost all my possessions I thought that I had nothing to give. Trees showed me otherwise. As I observed Tree standing in silence, rooted to one spot, I witnessed birds nesting on its branches, snakes gliding through its trunk, butterflies taking a break upon its trunk, squirrels sheltering inside it and children swinging from its branches. Tree gave to them all and sustained life for miles around it. It gave abundantly without taking one step in any direction or going out of its being to busily do-do-do. Just through its loving presence tree nurture life. This was a potent lesson for a recovering caretaker, workaholic and perfectionist like me!

Trees gift us with beauty, power and wisdom. They still our mind, center our soul, heal our body and energize our spirit.

They teach us that our power resides in our very presence, not in our possessions. Our presence carries all that we truly have and who we are. It speaks in silence, like the Poet-trees. As opposed to possessions, control and status —things that can be taken from us or disappear— the power in presence cannot be taken from us. This is the definition of power of the *Sacred Feminine*.

The poems in this book are expressed through words. But these words are uttered from the silence of the *Ancient Trees*, who teach us to speak from our soul and breathe powerful meaning into each word, instead of making incessant noise all day without truly communicating.

Trees are Ancient Healers

I wrote this book in the midst of adversity. I had lost all I had, all my art work, tools and materials, my finances, my home and my strength. I suffered from exhaustion, skin allergies and respiratory issues.

The loss came unexpectedly and showed me how fragile life is. Yet trees sustained me through the crisis. They helped me center myself. They modeled strength, stillness and patience. They were my companions, listening to me and letting me know that I was not alone.

They helped my respiratory system until I was breathing easy. They brought my heart into coherence, to transcend the crisis that had stressed me beyond my limits. They calmed my nervous system until my skin was glowing once again with health.

"These are growing pains," my tree friends would tell me when my pain and fear were overwhelming. They got me through the crisis. No. They did more than that. They helped me see the crisis as a gateway to a new life.

I regained my physical strength after several months of silent communion with my green healers.

The Poet-trees brought me back to wholeness while they inspired these poems.

Trees Return us to Our Belonging

When I listen to trees, I feel that I belong to *Pachamama*; that I am one of her children, one of her beautiful, wild creatures. This sense of belonging to Earth Mother, of being loved and being perfect just as we are is part of the healing that trees bring us.

So many of us are alone, alienated from the life around us and orphaned all the way to our soul. I call this epidemic of separation the *Orphanhood of the Soul*.

A long time ago, many of us were uprooted from our natural habitat to live in busy, noisy and contaminated cities.

Then this urban society dismantled the extended family as well as our local communities and neighborhoods. Even "The Company," —the old corporate workplace— which provided some belonging, has been sent overseas.

As a storyteller, performer and shaman, I have observed a heart-breaking change over the last 30 years. In group exercises and ceremonies, event participants exhibit increasing difficulty in connecting with others through eye contact. That's how estranged we are!

In these past years I've seen so many people depressed, lonely, separated and alienated. Their eyes carry a deep hunger and their skin is graying, as if they were becoming ghosts. Their soul is wilting.

You are a *Child of Gaea*. Go to *Gaea* and let her loving embrace nurture your *BodySoul*. You belong with the trees, the flowers, the plants, the creatures and the stars.

Go hang out with the trees. Miracles happen when you join the Poet-trees. You will begin to heal and you will experience Oneness.

The Journey in this Book

"The Tao of Trees" is a healing journey through the poems and naked bodies of the winter trees to find serenity and inner wisdom. Feel the love of *Pachamama* embracing you from the branches of trees and the flight of birds.

These poems were born from the silence and timelessness to which trees take us if we listen. They are teachings about life. They are the voice of the *Ancient Trees* taking us into a deep meditative journey. They breathe empty spaces into your mind and warm places into your heart.

These drawings came from being present with the trees, listening with my eyes and my body as well as my ears.

The presence of the trees speaks to us. Their shape and texture, their leaves, fruits and all the life dancing in and around them are part of their message. Just as our *Presence* is also a message to others. If we would only understand the gifts we organically bring through our very *Presence*, we would walk in grace. We would no longer struggle, stress out, suffer perfectionism or the anguish of obsessive doism.

There are so many gifts, so many healing messages and enlightening teachings that the Poet-trees gifted me that I could write this introduction for hours. But thankfully, the poems and the art will take you there.

Through these poems and drawings I pass on to you the gifts of Trees.

To receive these gifts, sit quietly and enter silence. Breathe slowly and deeply. If you can, sit by a window and look at a tree. Breathe with the tree.

Enter the *Tao of Trees*.

From my magical heart to your beautiful soul,

Maria Mar
The Dream Alchemist

Path of Beauty

The Poet-trees invite you to walk the Path of Beauty

See the beauty of the world and you will experience the magic of creation. Poetry is the language of your soul. Metaphor is not a figure of speech that poets created. It is the language of life, the language of the natural and sacred worlds. Life speaks to you in *Living Metaphors* that answer your questions and guide your choices. Beauty is one of the *Sacred Feminine Paths of the Heart* and its essence is harmony. Enjoy the magic expressed in all creation and your life will become a daily miracle, a constant celebration.

1

Poetry

Tree perches on Earth.
Bird perches on tree.
My eyes perch on bird.
Poetry perches on my eyes.
Spirit perches on poetry.
Earth holds Spirit
in this instance
of beauty.

2

Beauty

Why do I feel
ashamed of my own body?
This tree I see
is leafless, gnarled and grey,
like an old toothless, bride.
Yet it bares itself
with dignity to winter.
It is misshapen and dry,
yet
in every crooked branch
lies its beauty.
It is raw, unadorned,
and offers neither
shade nor shelter.
yet it is perfect.

3

Celebration

Yesterday I did not see this tree.
I was in a hurry and walk past it.
After all, it was just another tree
like the many lining my path.

Now I stop in wonder.
Rain drops hang from the naked limbs,
like diamonds glittering
in the fingers of creation.

Like fairies, they twinkle
inviting me to play and pray;
filling me with gratitude.

This trunk is no longer ordinary.
Father Winter's dazzling garland
has transformed this humble tree
into a celebration.

4

Awakening

The rain lulls me into sleep.
Blue mist
coils around trees,
devouring their solidity.
Blue mist
erases Earth's colors,
leaving behind
a faded landscape.
Heavy with moisture,
my eyelids almost close.
And with a blurry sigh
the landscape swirls and faints.
Maybe this is not real.
Maybe the trees are just a vision
that I dream up
to dress the barren Earth.

A sparrow appears
in a flicker of wings,
crowning the top of a tree,
opening my eyes.
So unpredictable it must be real.

TAO OF TREES

5

I have not yet heard a bird

I have not yet heard a bird
crying because it can't sing.

I have not yet seen a flower
wilt before it blossoms
from fear that its colors will not delight.

I have not yet followed a scent
that hid its essence in shame.

I have not yet touched a stone
that coiled, feeling not enough.

Yet, I have heard your silence
cry the truth that you betray.

And I have seen your beauty
wilt while you try to fix yourself.

I have missed the scent of your soul
from your words, your deeds, your work.

And I miss the touch of your presence
while you wait 'till another day
to do more and be more
stealing your fragrance from the world

Path of the Heart

The Poet-trees invite you to walk the Path of the Heart

The qualities of your heart are also the *Gifts of the Sacred Feminine* within you. The heart has a different way of knowing than the logical mind, and it is closer to the wisdom of trees and the mind of creation. Through your heart, you awaken the gifts of harmony, love, coherence, joy and delight, compassion and gratitude. Your heart generates the *Alchemy of Vulnerability* that allows you to transmute loss into love. Listen with your heart and you will hear the *Symphony of Creation*. Listen to your heart and you will find the compass that leads you to life's delight. Follow delight to the light!

6

Intimacy

Short Version

The distant wall of fog
silently advances,
becoming rain.
Now I can see the empty spaces
between each raindrop.
Now I can hear its song.

Long Version

The grey fog
renders the world around me
a cold, remote place
that chills me to the bones.
Not a bird sings.
Silence has swallowed
the familiar sounds of life.

The distant wall of fog
silently advances,
becoming rain.
Now I can see the empty spaces
between each raindrop.

My soul dances
in those empty spaces.
They are breathing spaces.
Raindrops bounce
against all surfaces,
little merry tap dancers.
Their rhythm reverberates
in my cells.
The world is no longer silent.
Now I can hear its song.

Which version do you prefer? Let me know at maria@shamansdance.com

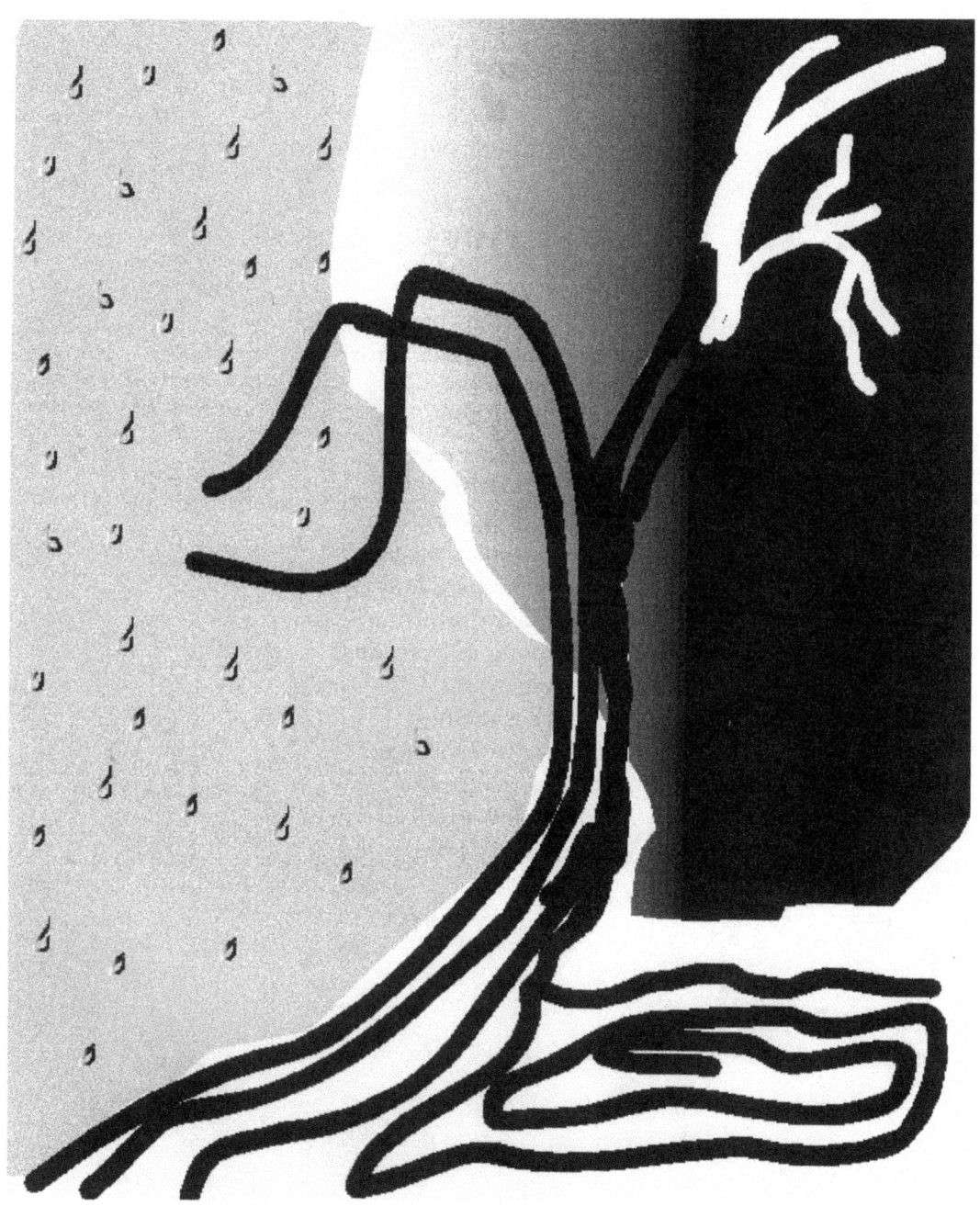

7

Love

Why are they back,
these stubborn black birds?
The winter winds
have blown their nests away.
There are no leaves
on the bare branches
to hide or shelter them.
Yet there stands the tree,
still giving, open, ready.
And birds return
to sing among its branches,
to perch on its warm, bare arms.
Love is the nest.
Presence is the shelter.
And birds return to trees
like the lover returns
to the Beloved.

Tao of Trees

8

Joy

Black birds upon white branches
merrily chirping away
tree's silence
jumping from the trampoline
of its warm stillness
into the cold pond of sky.

9

Dancing

Who says that trees can't dance
because they don't have feet?
This tree is grounded at its roots
and stillness holds its trunk below;
but as it gracefully opens its branches
to the space around,
this tree unfolds its dance
from within.
It rides in the spirit of the winds,
swinging from south to north,
from south to north,
changing directions, playing
with the breeze,
from east to west,
from east to west,
until it starts whirling of its own,
whirling, like the Sufi dancers,
a sacred dancer
spinning stillness into movement.
Who says that trees can't dance
because they don't have feet?
Tree dances with the rhythm of life,
for in the heart of every living being
there is a dance
born from stillness.

Tao of Trees

10

The Wounded Dancer

She stood gracefully in front of me,
her heart completely exposed.
It had been carved with a blunt knife
long ago by a ruthless lover.

She was exuberant and amazonic;
though others may have called her
misshapen, chubby or overweight.

The trunk of her body was short,
but her long arms
reached up to heaven
and blossomed
into graceful movements
that played with the bright sky above.

Out of her womb rose two long trunks,
making her a trilogy.

These trunks also rose
majestically into the sky,
like a stage star receiving an ovation.

Her roots immersed themselves
deep into the darkest,
most moist secrets of Earth,
absorbing her mysteries
to then sing them triumphantly
to the stars.

This I saw in the tree in front of me.
This she said into my Soul.
This she mirrored for me.
"Be triumphantly you!
Sing to the Sky
the song that runs
through your body,
a frequency rooted
in the deepest part of you!
Connect to Earth.
Let your heart and hers
beat as one!
Gracefully dance
your Wounded Heart
into healing!"

*What two qualities in our heart do the initials "M&J" carved in the tree heart stand for? The closest guess gets a free **Path of the Heart** digital art portfolio with the art from this section. Send your answers to maria@shamansdance.com*

Path of Co-creation

The Poet-trees invite you to walk the Path of Co-creation

Trees know that they are not alone. But humans have forgotten. You are not alone. You are not separate from creation. How does an animal know what fruits are toxic, where there is water or that a hunter is approaching? They are connected. They are in constant dialogue with creation. And so are you, but you have grown deaf. When you open your heart, mind and body to receive support, love and guidance, you meet your *Creation Partners*. Life becomes synchronous. Miracles are everywhere. And you co-create what now seems impossible by engaging the universe in and around you.

11

Trust

Deep into Earth
tree sinks,
surrendering to its inescapable pull.
High into sky
it rises, twisting and bending
without falling,
defying gravity.

Tao of Trees

12

Growth

Tree does not push or pull
neither tries nor fails.
Its growth is not measured
by accomplishments or endeavors.
Its force coils inside its heart
in an expanding
circle of life…
Accepting.
Allowing.
Acknowledging.
Appreciating.
Giving and receiving.
Holding and releasing.
Embracing the potential.
of that tiny seed
until it embodies its infinite love.
Stretching its capacity.
Gathering its potency.
…until tree shoots upwards
towards the stars.

Tao of Trees

13

Reciprocity

Even before tree is,
when it is only a dream of itself,
it feeds from the breast
of subterranean waters.
When tree finally bursts open
from the womb of Earth,
becoming the roots, trunk, leaves and fruits
that make it tree,
then it pulls down from above
waters to feed the waters.

As tree surges
it reaches up to sky,
grabbing ever expanding space,
ingesting oceans of carbon dioxide
and rivers of energy,
donning its shimmering light.

And as it soars,
tree gifts the heavens
the winged dances of birds
and their songs of delight.
It spreads its
leafy cushions of silence
so sky can rest its mind.

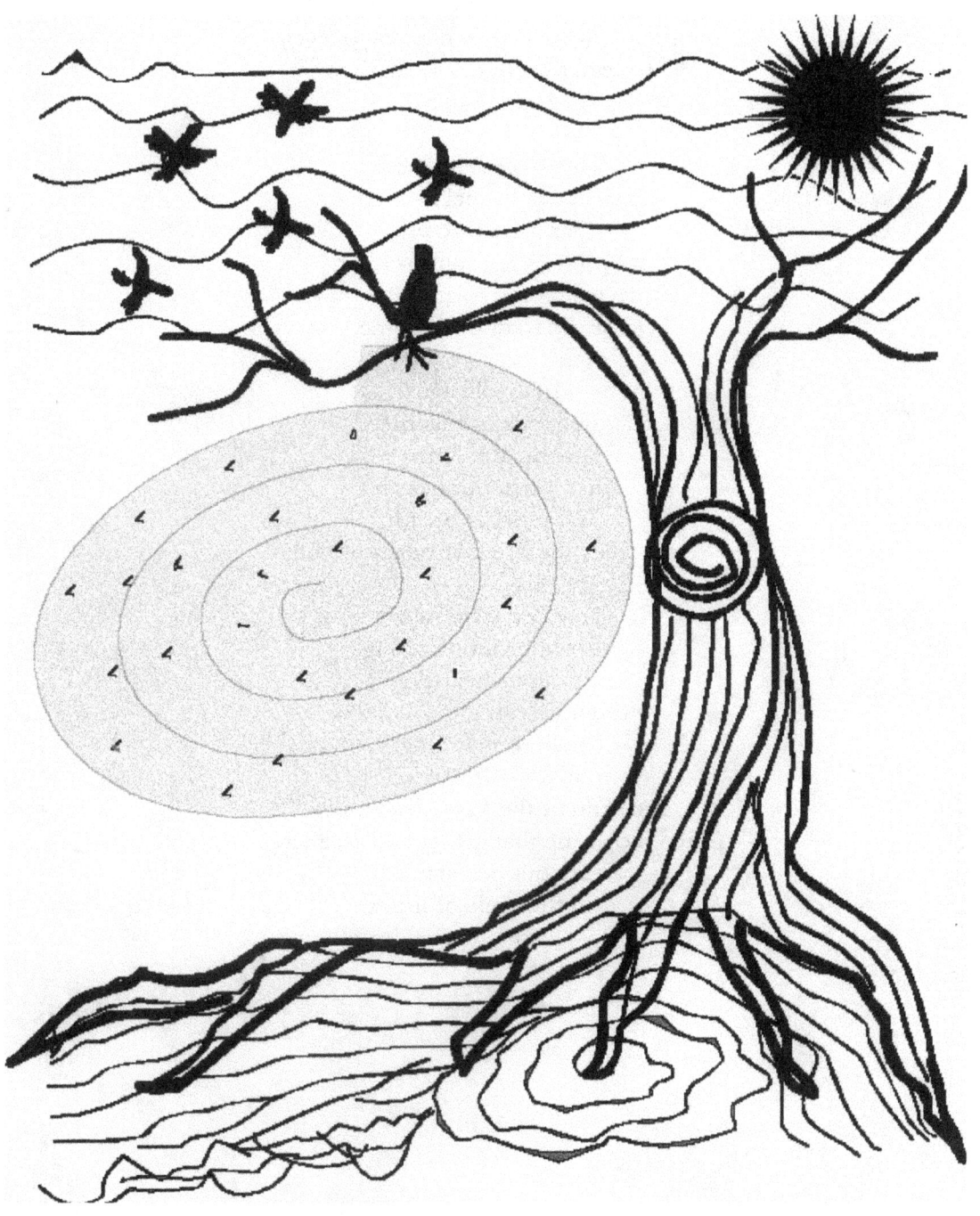

Even as it swings in the blue breeze,
tree generously exhales
luscious currents of life-giving oxygen
to feed the countless children
of Earth and Sky.

Tree draws sun's fire
into its belly to fuel its own life
and as it grows
it becomes the sun's scriber,
telling the solar story
for generations to come.

In its old age
tree returns this fire
in the dry limbs
that warm our hearth.
With its last breath,
tree feeds the fire that burns bright.

Tree keeps the secret
of giving and receiving
in its heart;
without greed or withholding,
guilt or grabbing,
timidity or excess.
Tree knows the *Law of Reciprocity*.
Tree shows me that giving and receiving
are but one action
in the cycle of life.

TAO OF TREES

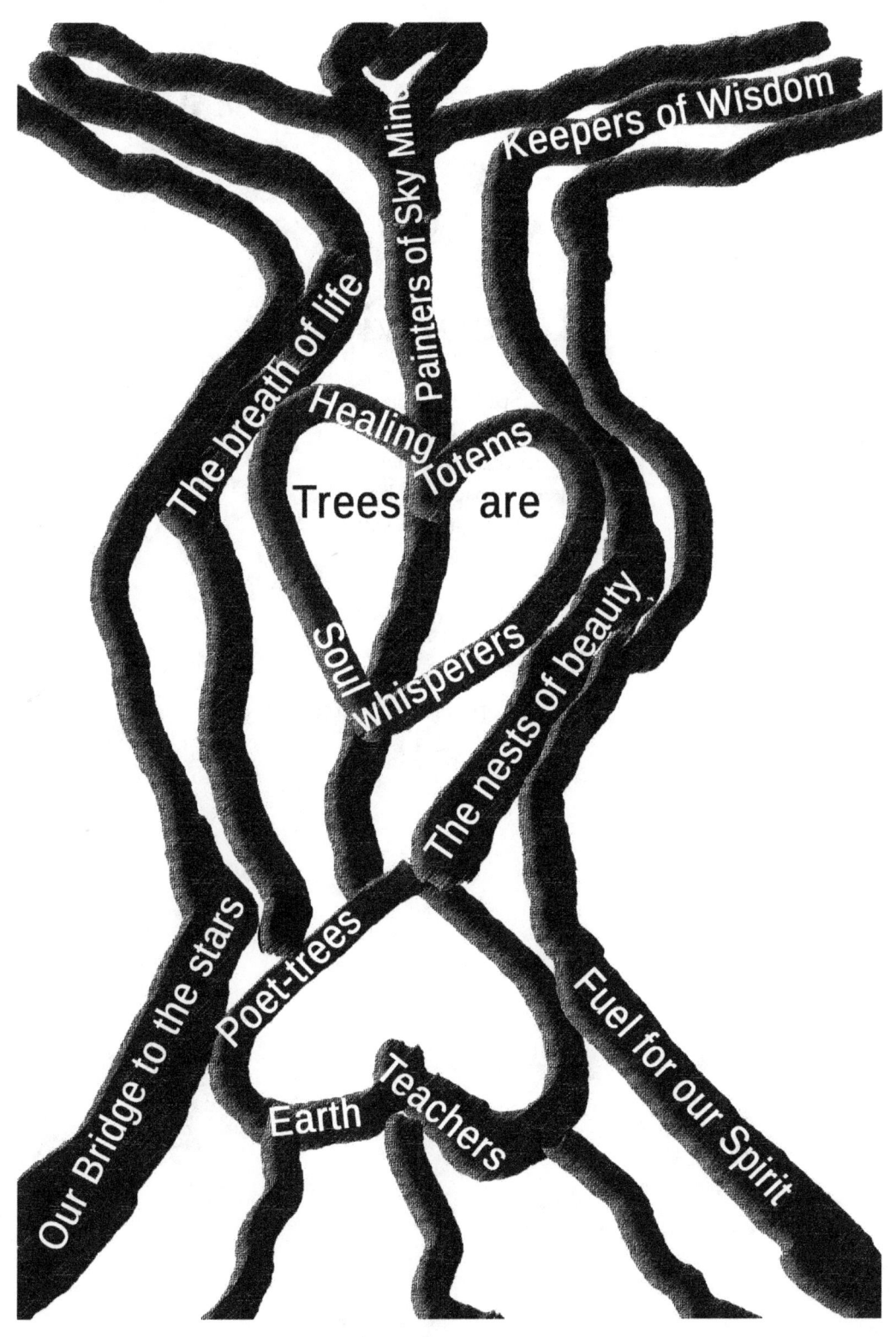

14

Receptivity

Spider-moon
weaves a web of radiance
in the emptiness
between those bare branches
reaching up to sky.

I look in wonder
at the shimmering garland.

A dazzling gift
to fit the open hand of tree.

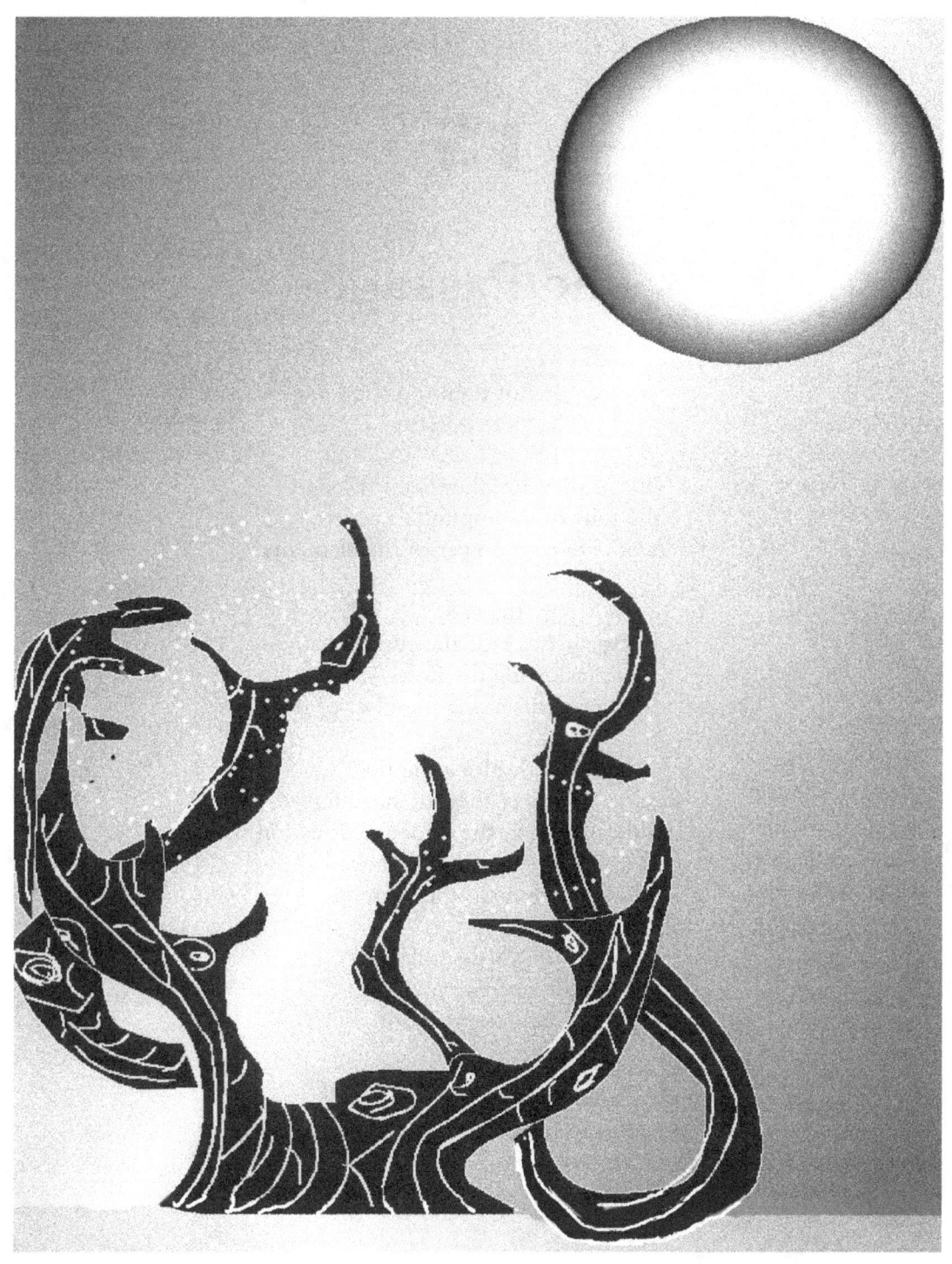

15

The Passage

Birds do not fight the wind.
They know better.

Tiny as they are, they acknowledge
the folly of attempting to control
the overwhelming power of the elements.

Instead,
birds gently ride the currents,
following the flow—
like the seamstress cuts along the fiber of the fabric.

Birds glide along the flow,
no matter where they are heading—
sometimes flying in the opposite direction,
seemingly lost or high jacked
by the whims of the currents.

But once inside the flow
birds find the passage
to their own destiny.

Tao of Trees

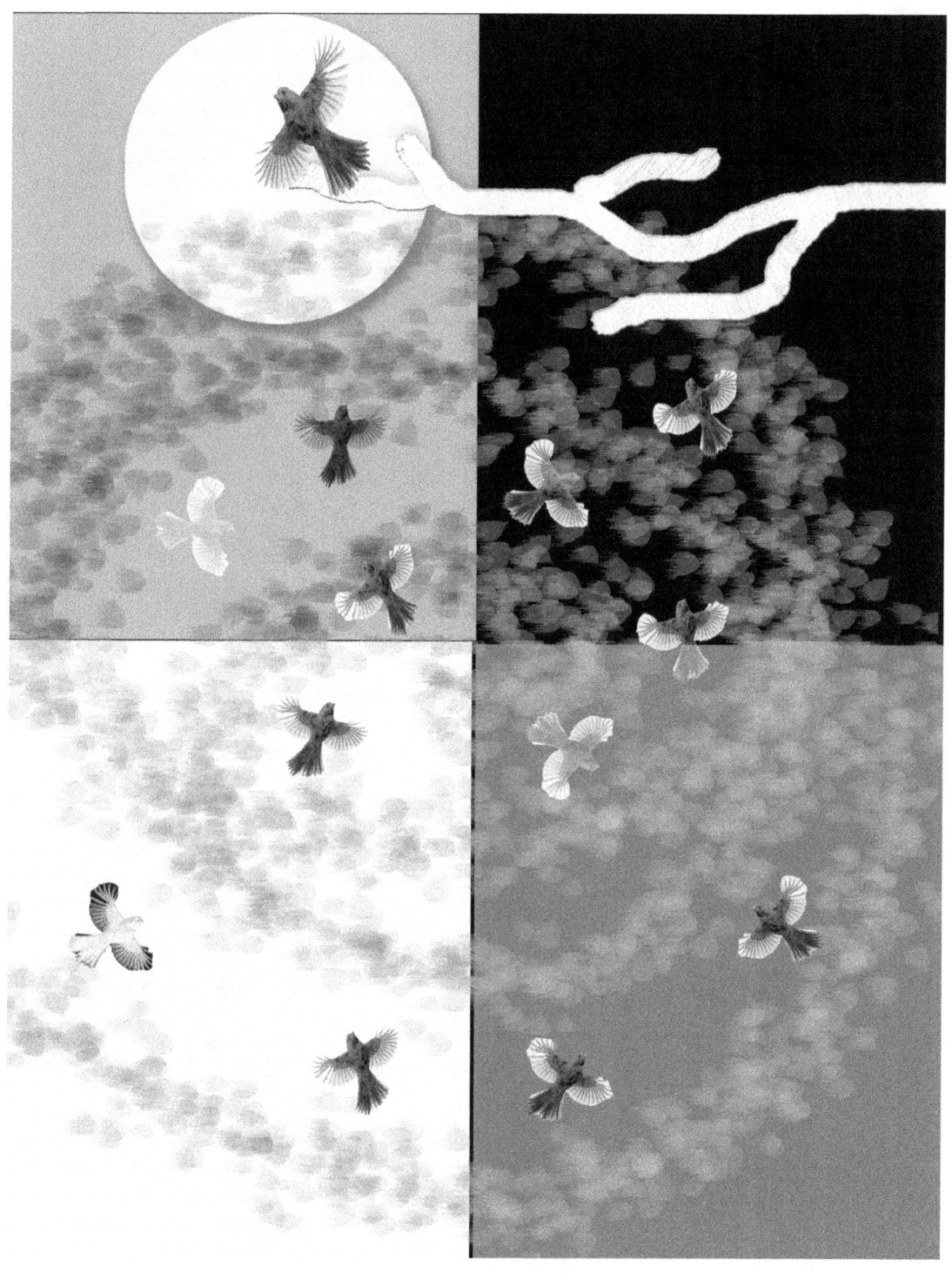

Path of Transformation

The Poet-trees invite you to walk the Path of Transformation

Life is flow in constant change —birth, growth, death, rebirth. When change stops, life stops. Entropy and stagnation lead to death. Life is transformation and the Poet-trees invite you to join the flow of life by walking the Path of Transformation. It is a path that demands courage. It is a *Warrior Path*. You wield the courage to shift your perception so that you can see with new eyes; for your perception creates your world. You wield the courage to walk into the unknown, for it is the path to renewal and growth. You wield the courage to walk through fear. You must take risks to become who you are and create what you want.

16

Attention

These trees have told me nothing
when I was not listening.
These trees have shown me nothing
when I was not looking.
That sunset did not linger
in those leaves,
did not paint with them this autumn sky.
Not one golden leaf
fell gently to the Earth.
Not one.

That dry, wrinkled leaf
did not crumble;
did not close upon itself.
It did not die, suspended,
in those stiff limbs
that caught this winter's snow.
These luscious green leaves
did not spring from
the warmth in the hearts
of those trunks
like kisses
from the lips of lovers.
Not one drop of rain
fell on a trembling leaf,
sensually gliding through its delicate veins.
Not one.
When I was paying
no attention.

Tao of Trees

17

Seeing

"Trees have no eyes,"
you say, little boy,
having been taught reality
by elders who have forgotten
the ancient art of Seeing.

Yet, full of eyes,
this tree's trunk
observes you quietly
and accepts your touch,
for it can see your innocence.

Full of eyes
this tree's roots
grasp life as it is born
in the dark womb of Earth.
It knows where water is,
what minerals to choose,
what life to make its own.
Full of eyes,
its branches firmly hold
the life that crawls and runs
and climbs and spins
in the vast space around it.

Full of eyes
its head reaches
for the sky
and with its light is crowned.

Trees have no eyes?

Have you heard of the ancient Seers,
who saw into the soul of man,
into the heart of nature,
into the realms of Gods,
into past, present and future?

Little boy, don't you know?
They were blind.

18

Opportunity

Catching the wind,
tree whistles.
Catching the light,
tree shimmers.
Catching my eye,
tree sees its own beauty.
Catching my attention,
tree dreams me.

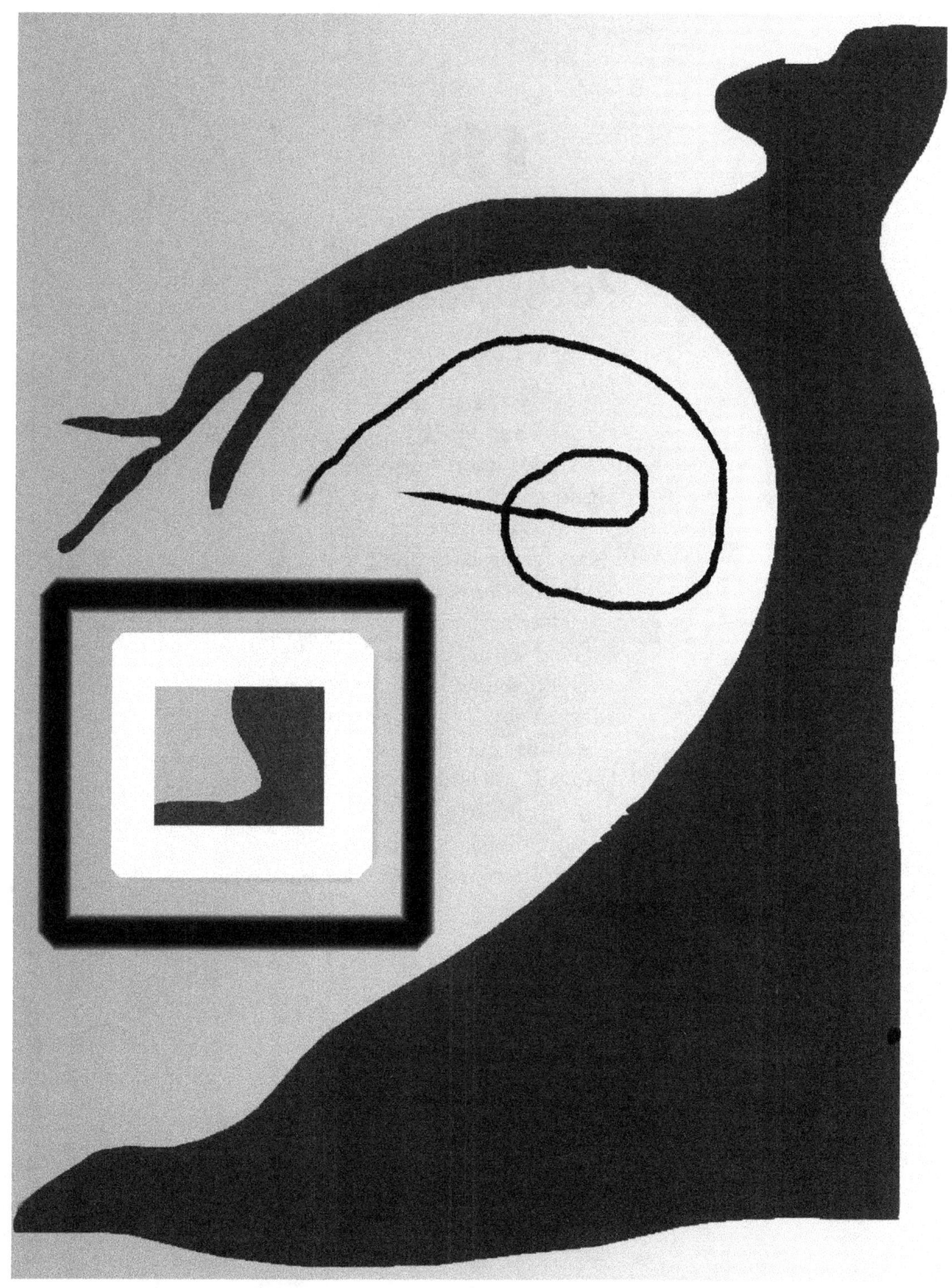

19

Persistence

One sparrow,
still and lonely,
held its stance upon this branch.
Rains came and went.
Mist drifted by.
Winds swayed it back and forth.
But this one sparrow,
wet and cold,
stayed on the branch.
I left the window
and went about my chores,
but this one sparrow
stayed, still and quiet,
all along.
And now there are so many,
a dozen sparrows or more!

Tao of Trees

20

Commitment

Howling winds run through you.
A siren in the distance
cries out against the gale.
Crow caws four times seven
and you are quite shaken
by the omen.

Roaring gusts run through you,
ripping out radiant rain drops
and deeply embedded leaves
from your raw skin.

A distant jet defies the sound barrier.
The sky is hard and grey,
like a menacing sword
above your head.

How can you still
hold that little sparrow
so tenderly on the tip of one finger?
How can the sparrow stay
so peacefully, balanced
on that gangly branch?

TAO OF TREES

Path of Presence

The Poet-trees invite you to walk the Path of Presence

When the wisdom of the *Sacred Feminine* was discarded humans began to create a lopsided culture where the power we seek is exclusionary, competitive and control-based. This is a definition of power when the *Sacred Masculine* is widowed from our *Sacred Feminine*. We suffer the consequences of that crippled power: compulsive consumerism, bullying, the destruction of our environment and a stressful, overwhelming life. The *Sacred Feminine* invites you to a definition of power as *Presence*. Everything you are and truly have is carried in your *Presence* and cannot be taken away. In *Presence* you are present here and now, inhabit your *BodySoul* and are connected to the natural and sacred worlds *The Path of Presence* reconnects you to your *Divine Self* while at the same time it restores your place as a child of Earth Mother.

21

Presence

Standing still
it bursts forth from the deep Earth,
opens its shell
and releases its potential.

Standing still
it reaches down to Earth's womb
and holds its molten power in its hands.

Standing still
it reaches up to sky
and grows to hear the stars.

Standing still
it harnesses the fire of sun
and channels the life force
of the waters.

Standing still
it grows long limbs,
green leaves and juicy fruits
that nurture life for miles
and miles around it.

Standing still
it harbors bushy squirrels
making home in its branches,
furry mice digging in and out
between its roots,
slippery snakes

TAO OF TREES

gliding around its trunk,
batty bats hanging upside down
like acrobats
and bees, butterflies,
monkeys, worms, ants
and million other life forms
all full of purpose,
madness and designs.

Standing still and silent
it bursts
with the laughter of children
on their swings
and the songs
of nightingales and larks.

Standing still,
without apparent movement,
it holds the flight of birds,
of beauty, dreams and poets.

Standing still,
not doing,
not controlling,
just being,
tree is the center
of life and death.
It participates.

Tao of Trees

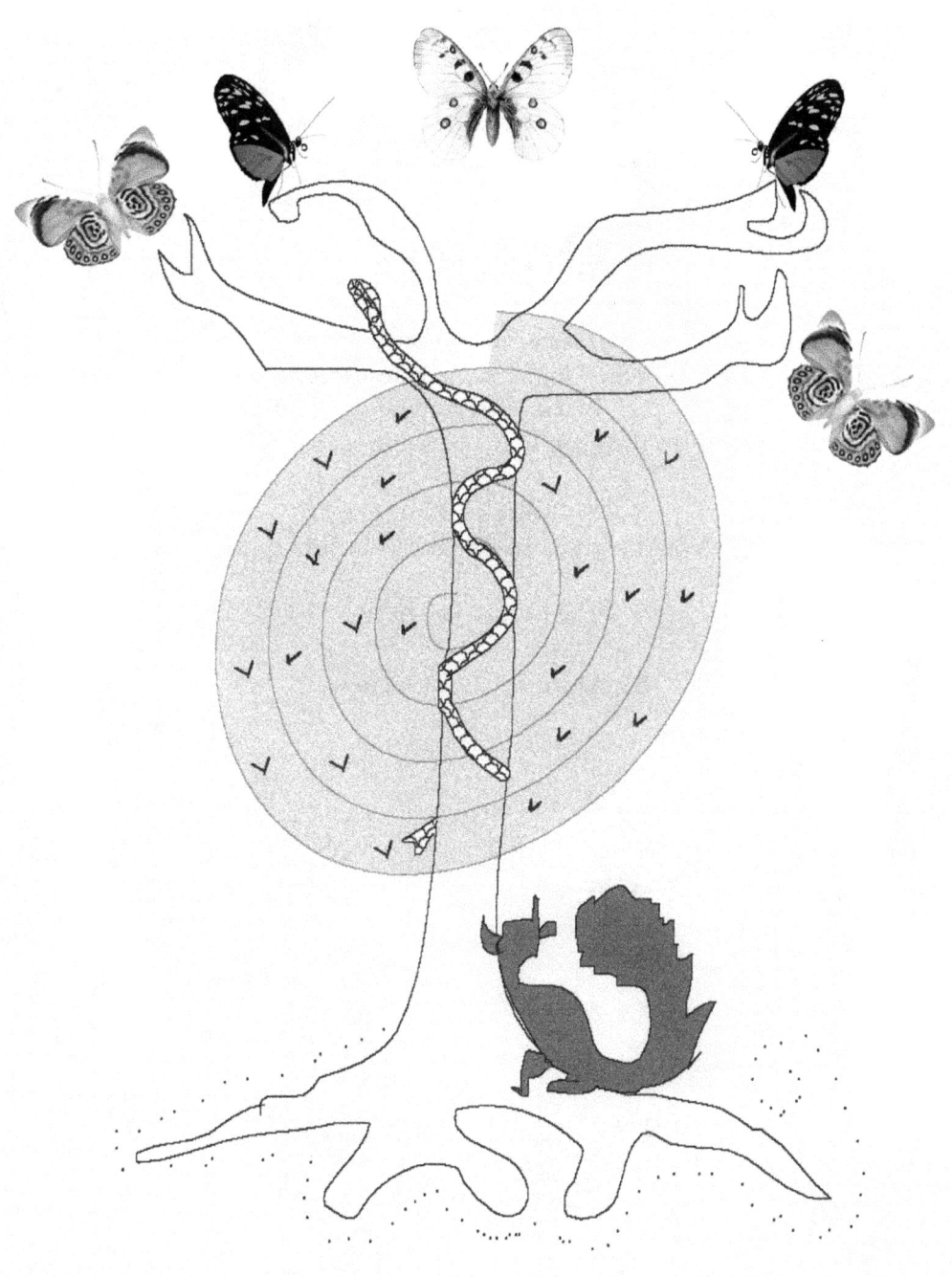

22

Oneness

Black bird, so tiny,
perched high on the tallest tree.
Black bird plunging
to the ground to eat some seeds.

"Black bird,
how could you see so far with your tiny eyes?"

"I see with the eyes of tree."

Blackbird masters Oneness.

23

Now

Lonely sparrow,
still and silent
like a sentinel of time,
grasping steadily
on to the fragile, trembling branch.

Watching the rain dissolve.
Mist drifting around the edges,
making everything so soft.

Seagulls spiraling above.

And now they are gone.

Tao of Trees

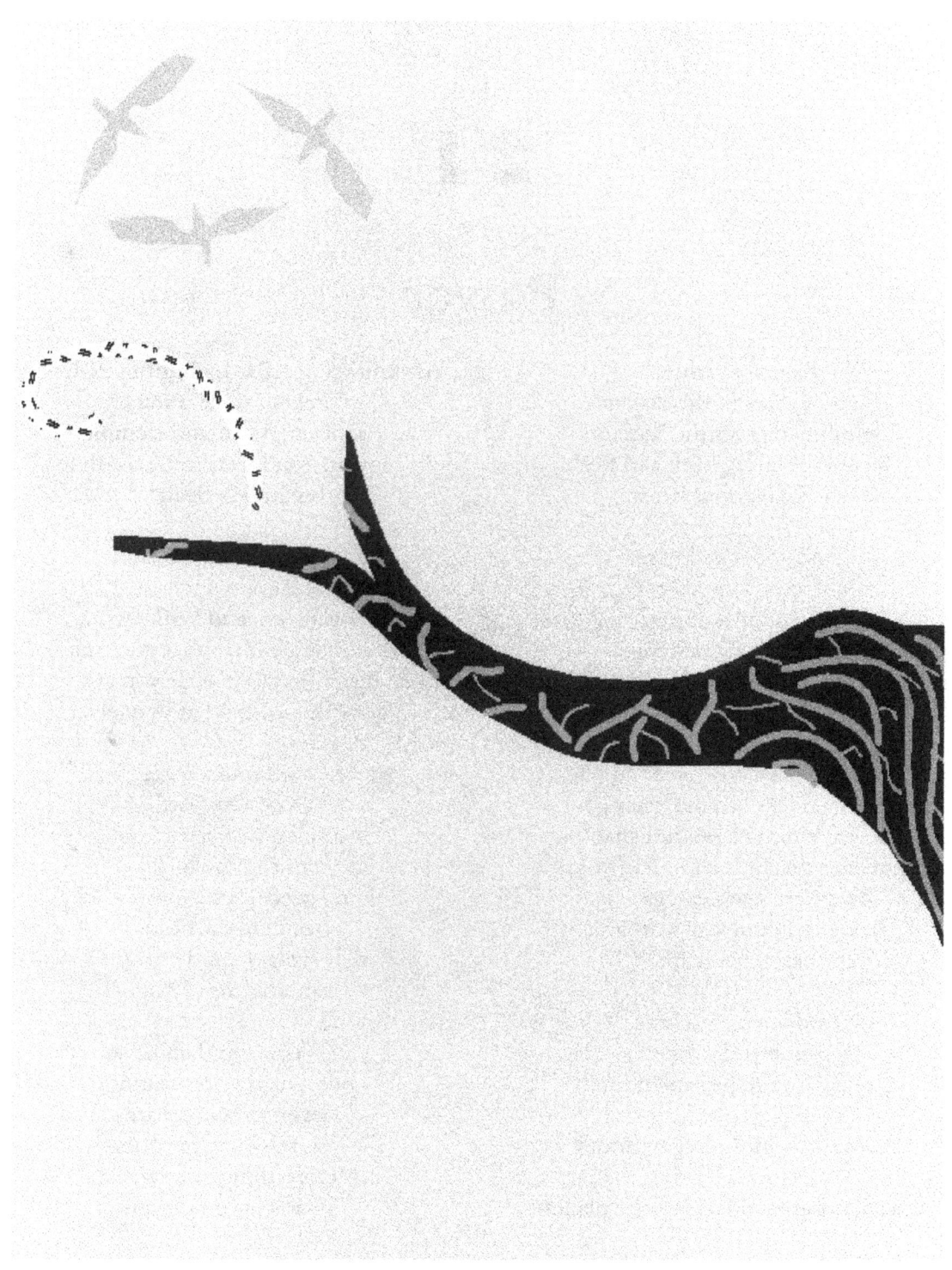

24

Power

Rain is starting.
Thunder roars in the distance.
Lightning pierces the horizon.
The cold is biting bark and flesh
like a ravenous beast.

And you stand here,
receiving it all,
afraid of nothing,
accepting everything,
as if nothing could break you,
as if everything supports you.

There are taller trees around you.
There are thicker trunks than yours.
There are more beautiful shapes,
more luscious branches than yours.
There are even evergreens
that should put you to shame,
bare as you are.

And you stand here,
proud and present
in all your naked splendor.

Above you birds sing harmony
into the world
and align the meridians of the planet.

Around you predators hunt mercilessly,
kings of their terrain.
Preys eat, listen and tremble.
Flowers can't wait to blossom in
breathless beauty.

And you stand here,
still and wingless,
clawless and leafless,
unconcerned by what you lack,
magnificent in what you are,
generous with what you have.

You stand here,
rooted to Earth,
waltzing with the clouds,
nesting the birds,
holding predators and prey alike,
shading the seeds
that struggle underground
waiting for spring.

You stand still,
but you are not waiting.
Everything you are
stands here *in* you.
Everything you have
stands here *with* you.

Tao of Trees

You fear not what may come;
for you are part of the dance of life,
a key player in the cycle
of birth, growth, blossoming, death and rebirth.
You do not compare yourself
with any other being or creature;
for you know that you are
an incomparable.

You surrender bravely
to the present moment,
relinquishing control
over the elements.
Yet, you stand here,
owning your power
to call in the elements,
to nurture life,
to cradle the Earth,
to ignite my dreams
and serve as a living antenna
to the stars.

You stand here,
inviting me to shine,
to free my brilliance,
to own my gifts,
to know my value,
to hold my power
in my presence,
to release control,
competition and compulsion;
for they are born
—not from power—
but from fear of inadequacy.

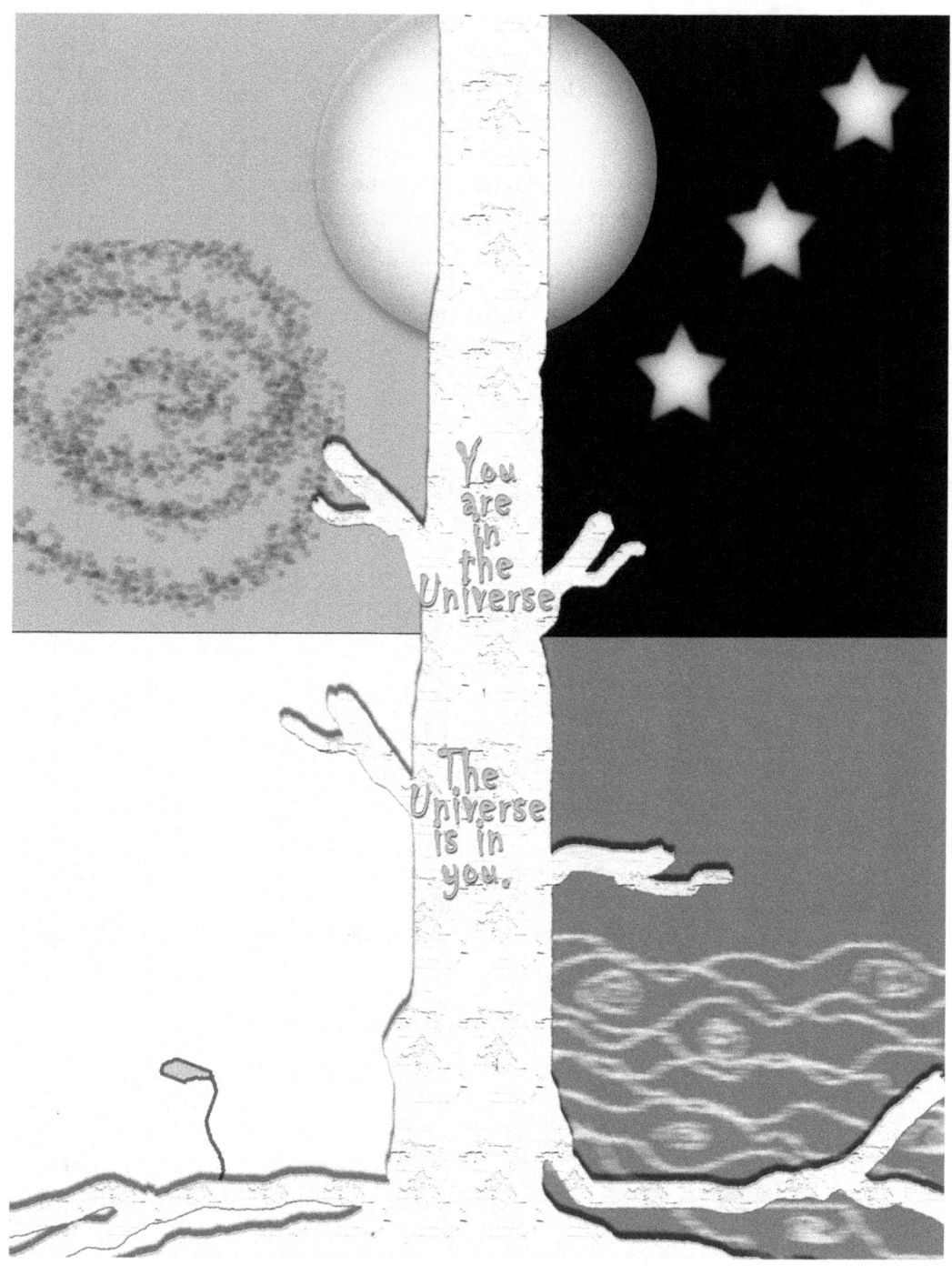

You invite me
to share my gifts
in my presence.

To stop "trying" and simply shine.
To stop struggling and join the dance.
To stop doubting and start giving.

To stop
controlling,
shrinking,
hiding,
shielding,
avoiding,
procrastinating,
fixing,
shelving,
competing,
and trying to excel…

And instead
to influence all of life
through the song of my soul,
the love that I am
and the fruits of my creation.

You invite me
to stand here,
in all my naked splendor.

Sacred Feminine Tree of Life

This art is also an oracle depicting feminine values in the Tree of Life and Death that the shaman uses to journey through dimensions. You can get a reading using this oracle if you are going through change, crisis or transition. See back pages.

25

The Trees are Smiling

The trees are smiling
with the resplendent
smile of bright green joy.

They smile because
they have been kissed
by the rain.
They have been caressed
by the sun.
They have been breastfed by Earth
and last night,
a full moon romanced
them until they tingled.

As I drink their luminous green
I too smile;
I'm being kissed by God's green lips.

My soles smile,
feeling supported and received by Earth.
They smile as they connect
to the roots of the *Ancient Trees*
and feel their warm welcome.

My womb smiles as it pulsates
with the life force of *Pachamama*
to create the world anew.

Tao of Trees

My heart smiles as it syncopates
with the Heart of the Earth,
overflowing with joy,
for I belong.
I am not alone.

I am one of Gaea's beloved creatures.

My lips smile with gratitude
for the verses that the Poet-trees
whisper into my Soul.

My eyes smile
with the beauty of creation.

My mind smiles.
Peaceful. Present.

Silent. Clear.
Not a cloud. Not a worry.
Sky Mind.

Path of Freedom

The Poet-trees invite you to walk the Path of Freedom

Freedom is about choice. This is also a *Warrior Path* from the *Sacred Masculine*. You were born into a culture, society or circumstance that may not support you in the ways you need in order to grow into your potential. You have no control over things that happen around you. But you do control how you respond to these situations. You can choose to give in or give up. Or you can choose to define yourself in ways that are congruent with your desires, dreams and potential. You can choose joy instead of despair. You can choose self-value instead of shame. As a human you have the ability to *Shapeshift* —to adapt, change and transform yourself and your perception in order to transform your interactions and ultimately your world. Every choice you make has consequences and moves you towards freedom or bondage.

26

Shapeshifting

Black bird
against white sky
perches
on a bare branch.
Wraps the sun rays
around its feathers
dismissing
the winter chill.
Becomes
a golden leaf.

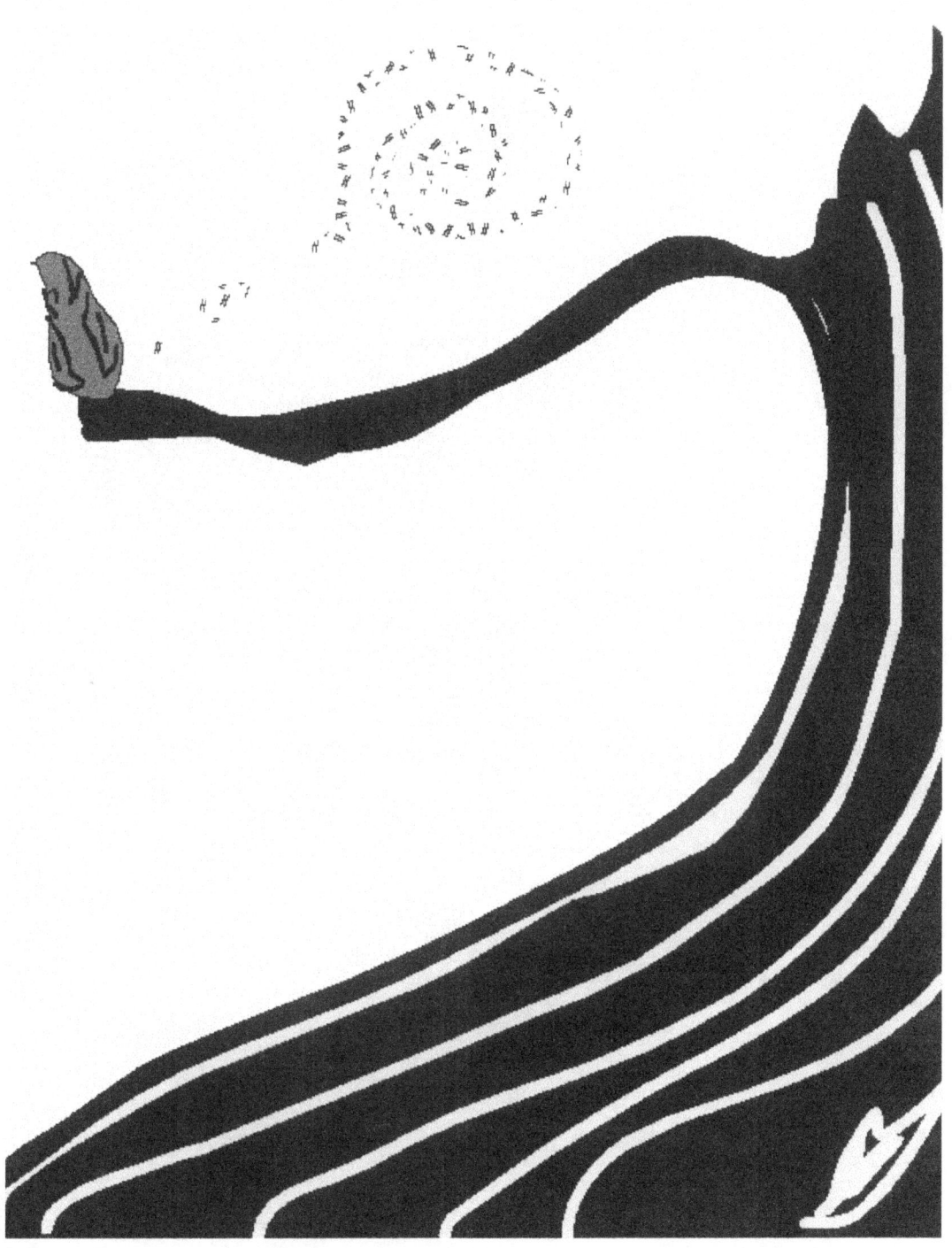

27

Non-attachment

Bird comes.
Bird goes.
Nest is built.
Nest is destroyed.
Leaves grow.
Leaves fall.
Tree opens its arms to life,
to creatures, large and small;
and just as easily and lovingly
Tree lets them go.
Rooted in Mother Life herself,
and living from its core,
Tree masters
non-attachment.

28

The Invitation

Like grieving widows
they stand,
dressed in black,
bathed in tears,
wrapped in the veil of mist.
Arms outstretched to heavens,
they do not cry for mercy
or beg to be relieved
of the harsh rains.
They do not ask "Oh, why?"
or rage against their fate.

Standing upright,
they gently beckon life.
They reach out
to the very heavens
that sent the storm
and open up, in trust.

Slowly one bird comes.
Two birds.
Three.

The storm is tamed
and sparkling rain drops
make the branches glow.
The winds no longer howl,
but sing with a jazzy,
raspy voice.

The sun cannot resist
the invitation.
Soon the widespread arms
are dressed in songs.

Like eager brides,
these trees now dance
in the light,
a gown of rhinestones
over their dark skin,
a diamond tiara
gleaming on their heads.

They slowly raise the veil
that covered their heads
to face *The Beloved*,
arms outstretched.

Poet-tree

You ARE your message.

What you seek
is who you are.

You are
shaped
by your
passion
for light,
rain,
wind and earth.

You show me that life
gives us not what we want,
but what we are.

29

Passion

The coldness of winter
has bore into their bark.
These trees stand upright and grey,
like shadows of themselves.

Suddenly the sun catches
the trees standing farther away.
They are illumined
in all their fine details; their golden trunks
adorned with subtle tones of brown and beige.
The warmth they exude
melts all sadness away.
Standing beside these enlightened trees,
the ones who have not
been kissed by the sun
seem to be in distress.

Passion is like this sun.
It seems to be
the very nature of a human being;
a force propelling her
towards what she desires.
Strength of intent,
irresistible warmth,
a lusciousness that is kin
to that of a forest when it rains;
(A lusciousness
which some mistake with lust.)
Yet it is simply the power of Spirit.

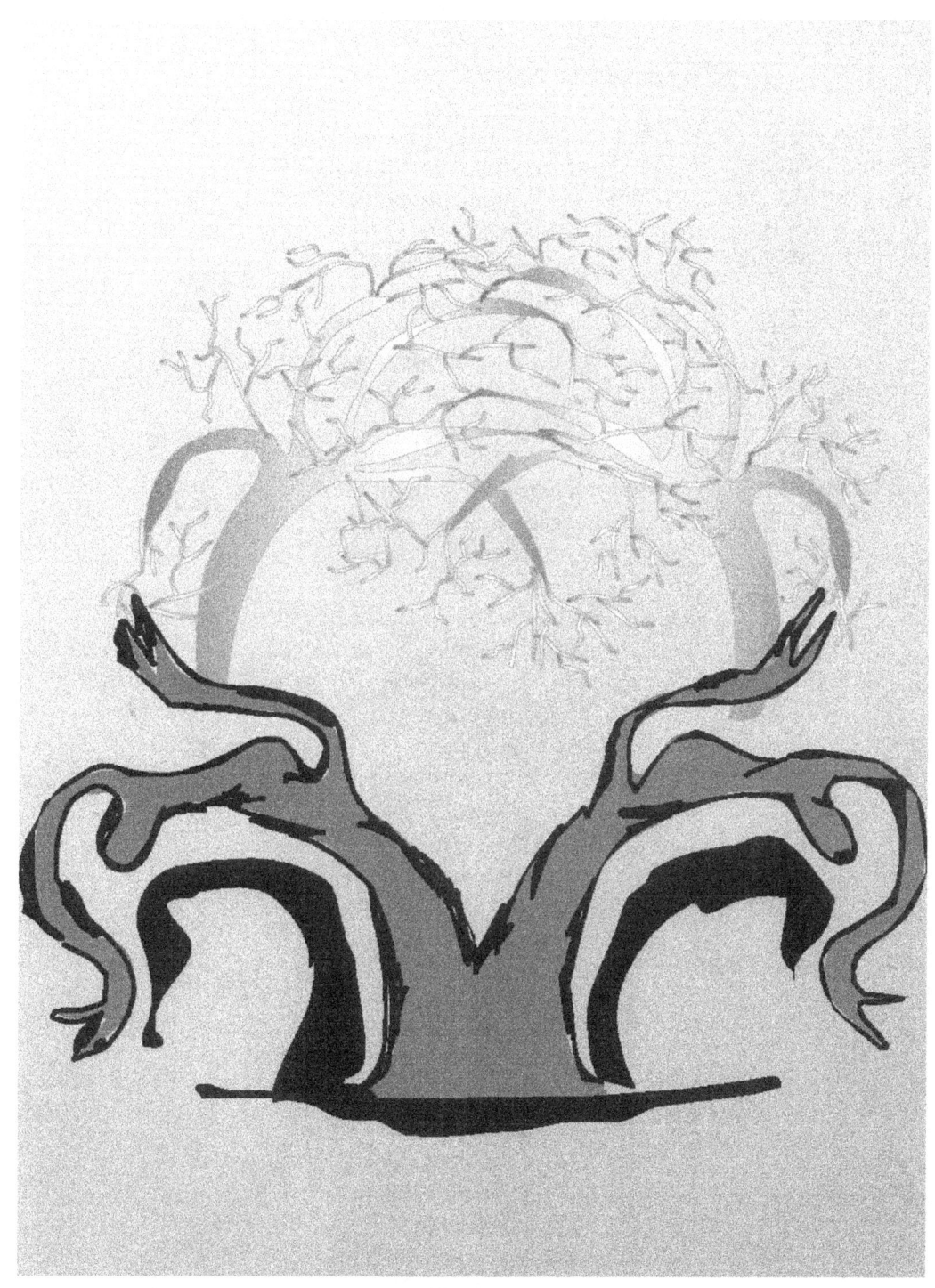

Life pours itself in her
and a woman opens her being,
letting its force run through,
enlivening her from within.

Life propels him forward,
and a man lets its force
be his instinct, his guide.

And when life wants
to pour out of them,
they again open their being
to let life's force burst out.

Passion is there, like the sun.
It appears suddenly, mysteriously.
But while trees just stand there
and receive it as it comes,
humans are free to receive it
or not.
Those who have not been kissed by life
are too shy, too wounded or too closed.
They have forgotten
the luminosity
inherent to their soul.
They have been battered
until they shut life out.
Perhaps they were planted
where the sun never shone.
Like the opaque trees,
they seem lifeless and dull.

But that is an illusion.
One subtle change
of perception,
an opening of the heart;
and they may
—like the dark trees
outside my window—
awaken to life
and glow in all their brilliance
once again.

Tao of Trees

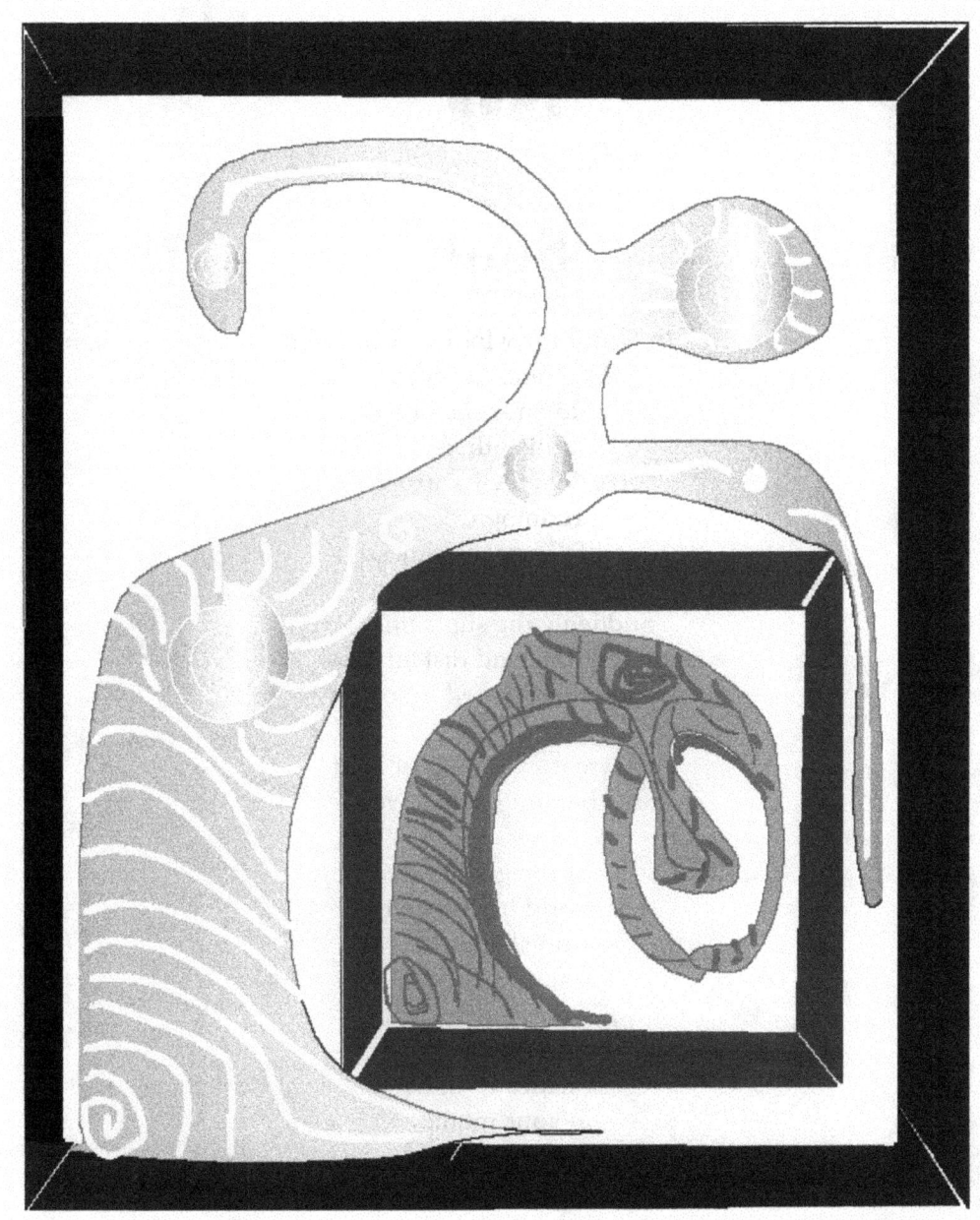

30

Soul

As I look out my window, I wonder:
Why does sadness
weigh down some people,
while others
unsaddle their sorrow,
running free
into life's expansiveness?

Suddenly the sun shines
upon the dark and distant trees,
turning their muted branches
into gold.
They are now a song of light
reverberating in my eyes.

The song of the golden trees says:
"The world has no colors,
no shapes.
It is all a mess
of light and shades.
An illusion.
A dance of light
in your retina.
At the core
of your perception
your souls speaks.
Its words paint the colors
and draw the shapes
of the world you create;
a world unlike any other."

What if we do not listen?" I wonder.

The trees closest to me
—still wrapped in darkness— answer.

"Darkness, too, shapes your world.
You project your own bitterness
upon the world
and then call it 'real'
and blame the world for it."

The dark trees invite me to look
from another window.
Their trunks —dark but a second ago—
are now beaming with warm light.

"What changed?" I ask.

"The angle from which you looked,"
answer the now sparkling trees.

"It is not your pain,
but your perception of that pain
which steals
the light from you."

"Then it is not sadness
which keeps the light out?" I ask.

"No."

Is it fear?

"No."

"Then what?" I want to know.

"It is disregarding your soul."

"How do I listen to Soul?" I ask.

"Change windows until you see the light."

Path of Healing

The Poet-trees invite you to walk the Path of Healing

The seventh and last path to which the Poet-trees invite you joins all the previous paths. It moves you towards harmony, which generates beauty. It is moved by love. This is not just a beautiful image. It is an axiom of *Energy Medicine*. Your *Spleen Meridian* is the Mother-healer energy within you. It activates all other meridians towards self-healing. It is strengthened by love. Disease calls upon your heart to activate the *Alchemy of Vulnerability*, allowing you to transmute loss into love and entropy into harmony. Healing reveals your breaking points —the places where you experience dissonance in your *Weave of Self*. Once healed these places become your strongest points. Healing leads you into a *Path of Transformation* that moves you into the *Path of Freedom*. No one likes to get sick. No one wants to feel pain or struggle with limitations. But if the *Path of Healing* sends you an invitation, seeing it merely as a struggle or seeing disease as weakness is missing the opportunity to clean open the old cracks in your *Weave of Self*, so that your radiance breaks through. What if you see healing as alchemy?

31

Meeting Pain

Trees bare themselves
to the harsh, cold winter.
They surrender to the pain
of cold winds and freezing rains
knowing that a fresh new Earth
awaits them.

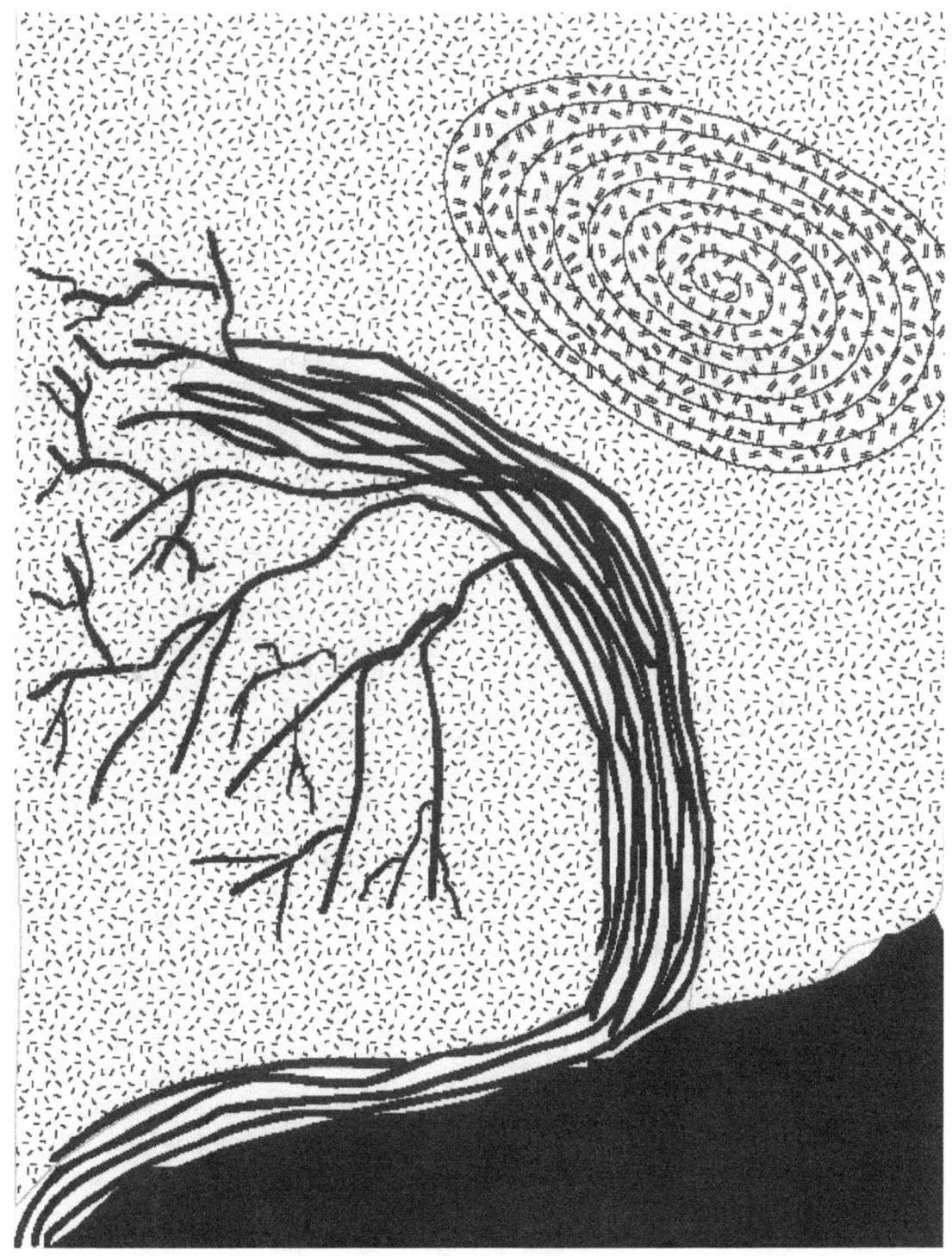

32

Cleansing

Pure crystals shimmer
against the light,
dancing frantically
as they fall
upon the dark, dry Earth.

It is a solemn moment.
The world is now a temple.
We grow quiet
—as in prayer.
We hear the silent fingers
of snowflakes as they baste
tiny stitches,
weaving a giant new blanket
over the naked Earth.

The trees grow pale
under the snow.
They are in the midst
of a cosmic cleansing.

The Yoruba priestess
cleanses her subject
from bad energy
by sweeping the body
with a white dove
that collects the toxins.
When the dove flies away
it takes the evil with it.

The snowflakes
are the falling feathers
of a giant white dove
sweeping the world clean.
When will the darkness fly away?

It is hard to walk
through the deep snow.
It is dangerous to be careless
while transversing
its treacherous luminescence.

Not everything in snow
is as soft as it looks.
Underneath its layers,
at the borders of its pliability,
rise deadly sharp edges.
One can fall and get broken
against these icy blades.

Like some promises,
this smooth brightness
hides a wounding frame.

At these mysterious moments
It is best to turn inwards.

Stay inside,
where it is warm, dry and familiar.

From the clear window,
detached from the
inclement snow storm,
one can see its impeccable beauty.
One can enter its sacred silence.

One can see what remained invisible
and hear the silent truth
that had been drown in the
tempest of routine.

Yet, it may be necessary
to sink into the deep softness outside
and get thoroughly wet.
It may be inevitable
to stand right in the middle
of its chaos
and let the violent white winds
batter the old stagnant stories
from our cells.
It may be essential
to face the storm
standing at its center.

After the storm
the air is pure.
Trees glow,
as if they had spent
a whole night
making love.

The mind is clean and vast.

There is an instant then
—after the last snow flake falls—
when you can feel
the seed of life
pulsating deep in the heart
of the warm, wet Earth.

It beacons.

I am storm.
Thundering into your bones.
I am ghastly winds
battering your body
with ghostly howling
haunting your nerves.

I am blasting bullets
of raindrops
badgering your muscles.

I am crisis.
Disaster.
Aggravation.
Irritation
Obstacles
Opposition.
Lack.
Oppression.
Struggle.

I am storm,
cleansing away
the old carcasses of the past
and renewing your atoms.

I am possibility.
I am renewal.
I am transformation.

You decide.

Listen deeper.
The heart of the warm Earth
beats as one with your heart.

Listen deeper.
Feel life bursting through you.

Let yourself blossom.

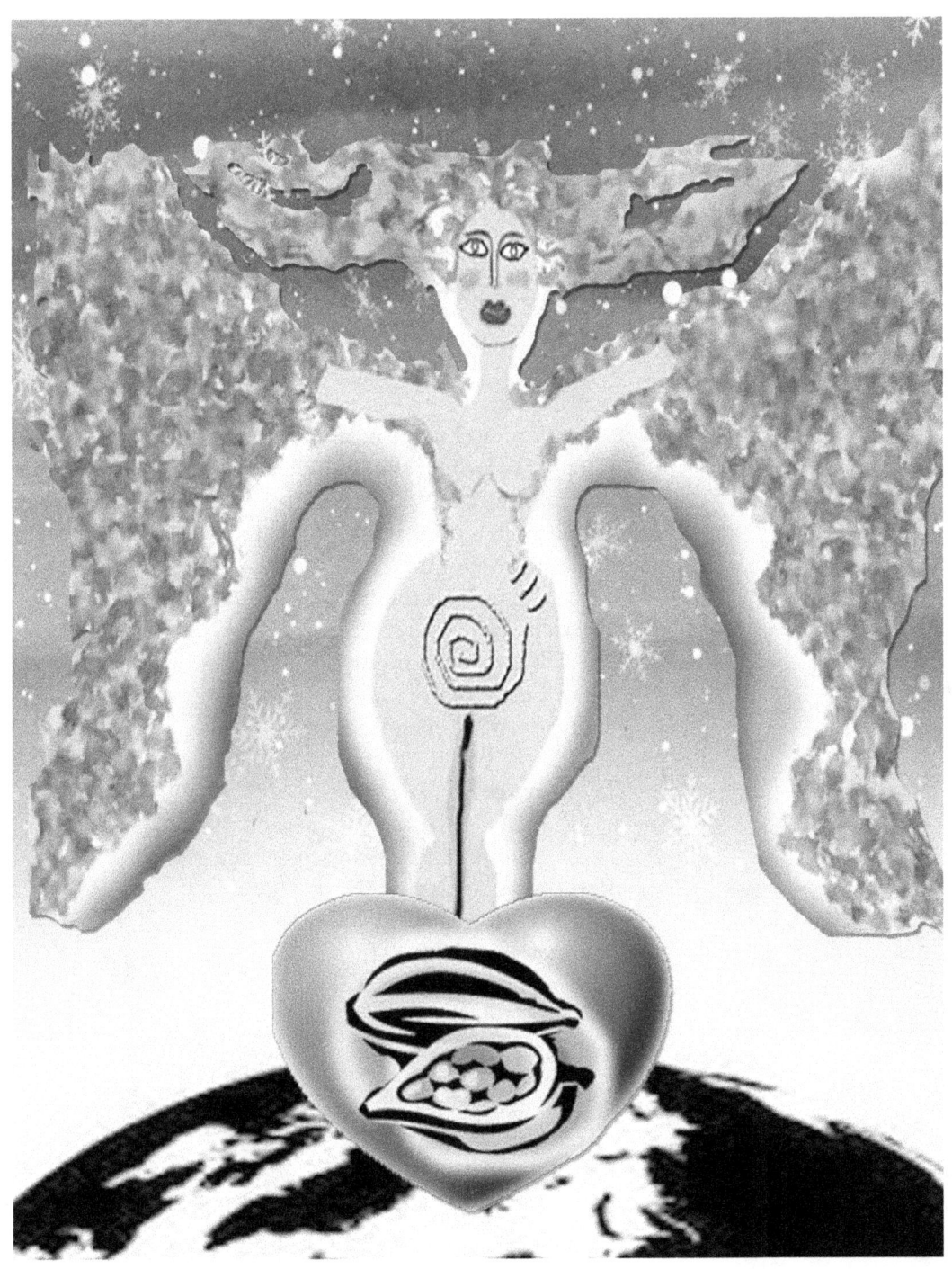

33

A Higher Dance

The trees are no longer naked.
The wind swept through the branches
spreading a shower of white sequins
that dressed them in a radiant white gown.
They are so elegant now!
I could shiver with the cold.
But the trees invite me to dance,
and their dance keeps me warm.
And their beauty…
Oh! Their beauty, so magnificent…

The presence of *The Divine*.

As in my life,
it often shows up as tiny drops
that hurt as they jab and stab,
piercing my comfort,
making me shake.
Only later do I see
the miracle that redressed
my nakedness,
the gown that makes me ready
for a higher dance.

34

The Messenger of Hope

There is a Goddess living in that crack.
That wound you carry is sacred.
That scratch, that lump, that burning pain,
that toxic, damaging rubbish inside you,
the illness you resent and see
as your enemy and destruction
is a threshold into your *Unique Essence*;
a key into your Life Purpose;
a guide into your deepest truth.

You see it all the time.

The field is plastered in cement.
The yard is covered in debris.
All life seems to be dead and buried.
Then, out of the smallest crack,
the fresh, green shoot emerges.

It is the Messenger of Hope.
Your Hope.

Its message blossoms in its leaves:

You have the power to heal anything.

Resource Section

This section contains resources you can use to enrich your reading of this book, from the audio meditations to the art portfolio.

It also explains how you can join our **Tree Love Campaigns** to participate in saving trees around the world.

This section also features events that go with the poems for organizations and presenters. You can also find out about bulk orders and other options here.

Finally, I've listed organizations, websites and articles that help you live a tree-friendly life.

Tree Love Campaigns

Become a Street Team Member

If you want to join the **Tree Love Campaigns** that allow this book to contribute to saving trees and healing our beautiful earth, please join by visiting the web address at the bottom of this page.

We will notify you of the next book launch campaign.

Our campaigns usually coincide with Earth Day, Arbor Day and National Tree Day in the USA.

Each of us —no matter how shy or private— has the potential to reach thousands of people through word of mouth. By partnering as a *Street Team Member* in these tree-saving campaigns, you spread consciousness about the importance of saving our trees throughout the world. You also help us raise funds to save trees.

$5 from each book sales goes to saving trees and is donated to different tree-saving organizations who partner with us for each campaign. Larger amounts are donated from art portfolios and other offers connected to the book.

This book and the **Tree Love Campaigns** are my way of saying thanks to the trees that give me life and brought me back to health.

You can give thanks to the trees by joining our **Street Team** —no matter where you live.

http://dreamalchemist.com/tao-street-team

Tree Love Campaigns
Become a Campaign Sponsor

As a business owner, corporate leader or institutional decision-maker, you have the power to bring the **Tree Love Campaigns** to your clients, staff or members. When you do this, you:

- Spread inner peace, harmony and beauty in your environment,

- Help in the self-healing process of your people,

- Contribute significantly to our goals of connecting people with trees, saving trees and earth, and

- Generate a deeper connection with, gratitude from and a positive brand in your community.

Our campaigns usually coincide with Earth Day, Arbor Day and National Tree Day in the USA. When you become a *Campaign Sponsor* you have options.

- **Institutional Package:** Purchase a bulk order of books and/or audios and place them in your corporate bag for a special occasion.

- **Institutional Event package:** Purchase an Institutional Package with a special event for your community, staff or members.

- **Seasonal Sponsorship:** Sponsor a season in our **Tree Love Campaign**. Your branding as sponsor will be significantly displayed.

- **Annual Sponsorship:** Sponsor a year in our **Tree Love Campaign.** Your branding as sponsor will be significantly displayed.

http://dreamalchemist.com/tao-sponsor

If you want to listen to these poems...

Tao of Trees Poetry Meditations
in the voice of poet-shaman Maria Mar

The Tao of Trees Poetry Meditations allow you to journey through the *Tao of Trees*.

- Listen to the healing voice of poet-shaman Maria Mar as she takes you into a relaxing meditative journey through the *Tao of Trees*.
- Each poem comes to life in Maria's voice enriched by meditative sounds, such as the Tibetan Bowl, spirit chimes, rain stick, African wood marimba and other instruments that calm your heart and bring peace to your mind.
- Seven Paths. Seven tracks.
- MP3 format.
- Immediately downloadable

$5 from each sale goes to saving trees

The audio meditations will be released during Tree Love Campaign for National Tree Day at the end of July, 2018.

Pre-order now
You will not be charged until the audio is available.

https://gumroad.com/l/taotrees-audio

Get a Tao of Life Reading!

The Sacred Feminine Tree of Life is an illustration. It is also a totem representing the shaman's *Tree of Life* envisioned by Maria Mar to honor the *Sacred Feminine*. Whether you are a woman or a man, you can get a personal reading by Maria Mar. This reading focuses on:

- **The cycles of life**: birth, growth, blossoming, death and rebirth, as it pertains to your life and to specific goals, dreams or issues. What is trying to be born through you? What are you birthing in what is dying? What needs to be released? What is struggling to blossom in your life right now? How can you bloom where you are planted? How can you feed your dreams and talents? What old story is calling you to rebirth by rewriting it into the story of you living your brilliance?

- **Your shamanic travel map.** Which of the worlds in the shaman's *Tree of Life and Death* should you visit in order to solve the pressing issue? Where can you find your allies? In the Heavens Upper World, the Earth Upper World, the Middle World, in the Water Dream World or Lower World?

- **The Transformation Transportation:** How is the crisis you face right now a a portal to the life you want? What transformation is contained in your obstacle? How is that transformation the transportation to your desired destination? Reframe your current crisis and transform that wall into a portal to new possibilities and a bridge to your Dream.

Go to: **https://gumroad.com/l/tao-life-reading**

Tao of Trees
Portfolio

Create an oasis of beauty and mindfulness in your home or work environment and inspire your community to save our trees.

If you liked the illustrations in this book, you can purchase your personalized portfolio with digitally signed copies and one additional free print with your name on it, with my thanks for helping save our trees.

- The illustrations for each path are gathered in a portfolio. Choose the path you enjoyed the most and download the portfolio for that path.
- Each portfolio contains high quality black and white 8"X10" digital prints that you can print in any laser or inkjet printer, frame and hang in your home or office.
- You can choose the *Full Portfolio* that includes all the images.
- *Business Licenses* and *Corporate Licenses* are available if you are interested in using the illustrations for your book, website or products.

$5 or more from each portfolio sales goes to saving the trees.

Go to: **https://gumroad.com/l/tao-portfolio**

The Tao of Trees

Live Poetry Journey

The Tao of Trees is available as a deeply relaxing multi-media live poetry journey that takes you into the silence in your soul, creates Sky Mind and then connects you to the trees to heal body and soul, return to harmony and see life anew.

Visit the web address below to set a live face-to-face meeting to present this event at your site or event. *No obligation.*

http://dreamalchemist.com/tao-presenter

You can also email us at **shamansdancepublishing@gmail.com**

Bulk Rate Orders

The **Tao of Trees** is a healing journey that can be expanded into a collective experience or ceremony. When you purchase bulk rate orders, Maria shows her appreciation through online and local events, bonus gifts for your members and other special treats. These experiences are great for:

- Small and large Book Clubs
- Local libraries
- Websites or events that offer online group gatherings
- College classrooms and events
- Magazines wanting to offer a special treat to their readers
- Ecological organizations, clubs, websites and events
- Yoga, Taoists, shamanic, meditation or Buddhist organizations or groups
- Online businesses, coaches and services, websites and blogs as a special event, gift or sponsorship.
- Corporations wanting to treat their staff or help save trees during a special online, national or local event.

There is space for bulk orders as small as 10 books to orders into the thousands. We will talk with you and together we'll find the best fit for your needs and audience.

Email me at **shamansdancepublishing@gmail.com** to set up a live, face-to-face conversation and see how you can help save trees while the **Tao of Trees** helps you inspire your members and clients.

Save the Tree Resources

Learn more and volunteer with local or online organizations

- **Treepeople.org**
  Learn 22 benefits that trees give us and join TreePeople.org to save the trees. They are located in LA. Visit online at: https://www.treepeople.org/tree-benefits

- **Find resources for you to educate your community at** *Spirit of Trees*, a resource for therapists, educators, environmentalists, storytellers and tree lovers at: **http://spiritoftrees.org/**

- **Tree Conservation ideas, resources and activities from topiarytree.net**
  https://topiarytree.net/resource-center/tree_conservation.html

- **American Forests** has a beautiful site with great images, articles, activities and resources at: **http://www.americanforests.org/**

- **The Rainforest Alliance** has well-written articles and educational resources, videos and up-to-date news. It also promotes current campaigns to save our rainforests. Visit it at: **https://www.rainforest-alliance.org/**

Articles to help you save trees

It's important to know how to present the problem and what solutions are available in order to change the conversation and educate your community. These articles help you do that.

- **50 easy ways to save the planet**
  https://www.theguardian.com/environment/2002/aug/22/worldsummit2002.earth21

- **Why save Trees?**
  http://terrecon.com/why-save-trees/

- **How you can help save forests** (Includes links to resources and adopting a tree). http://www.green-organic-world.com/forest-conservation.html

- **Arbor Day Blog** has lots of beautiful and inspiring articles about trees. Enjoy them at: **http://arbordayblog.org/**

Practical things to do:

- **Buy tree-free paper products** made from grass and bamboo which grow back fast. Buy or learn more here: **http://cabooproducts.com/products/**

- **Do your printing in tree-free and 100% recycled papers.** Buy at amazon here: **https://www.amazon.com/TreeFrog-100-Friendly-Paper-793573849148/dp/B00BQX0EYW**

- **Buy banana paper and other products from Ecopaper.** Check it at: http://www.ecopaper.com/banana-paper-500-sheet-ream.html

- **15 practical things you can do** (or not) to save trees: https://livegreen.recyclebank.com/15-Ways-to-Save-a-Tree

- **25 fabulous ways to protect trees and conserve our forests** at: https://www.conserve-energy-future.com/fabulous-ways-to-protect-trees-and-conserve-forests.php

- **7 ways for kids to save trees** at: http://goexplorenature.com/2013/04/7-ways-kids-can-help-save-trees.html

- Join our Tree Love Campaigns!
  Sign up here: **http://dreamalchemist.com/tao-street-team**

Raise Funds and Spread Tree love!

If you are a tree-saving organization or event or an ecological website or campaign, you can join our **Tree Love Campaign** and raise funds for your organization.

You can also partner with us to use the book as a fundraiser for your campaign.

It's easy and quick and you don't need a special staff or expensive resources to do it.

Email me at: **shamansdancepublishing@gmail.com** for how to become one of the organizations that benefit from the sales of **The Tao of Trees.**

Find more information request a meeting here:
http://dreamalchemist.com/tao-partners

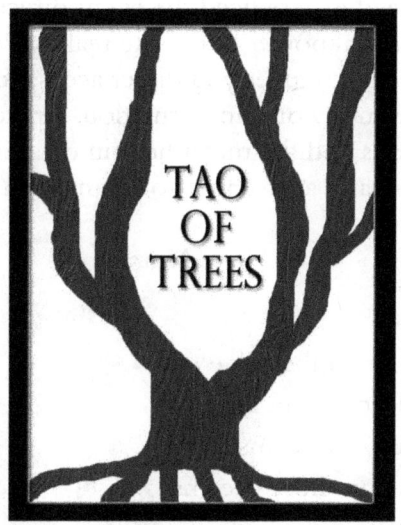

About Section

In this section you will learn more about the author and where to find her. Discover other books by Maria Mar. Subscribe to enjoy future books by Maria. Find out about Maria Mar as a speaker or presenter for your organization.

About Maria Mar

"Stories are the only imagined structure that can lay down actual memories, as if you had experienced the event directly in real life. This gives story the alchemical power to rewrite reality. Poetry is the language of the universe. It gives you direct access to your *BodySoul*. It can be an instant ceremony of transformation. Art reveals and transforms the patterns and the metaphors in creation. That's what I do. I use story, poetry and art to help you transform your world, starting with yourself."

~Maria Mar~

As far back as I can remember, I've been nurturing people's right to dream and make their Dreams come true —Dreams, with capital D— for I'm interested in those dreams that make you come alive, that unclip your wings and fill your heart with overflowing joy. Dreams with small letters —those that stay solely at the acquisition level, including only things; like a car, money or a house— are in my eyes consumerist illusions. There's nothing wrong with wanting those things. But you came here at this time and in this place to unfold your potential and help others do the same. You can obtain the things you want or need as the natural outcome of your bigger Dream, the one that connects you to your BIG Why. That's the one I help you bring to life.

This desire to nurture people's creative potential and help birth their Dream started with my grandma's poems; the ones she burned to get "tough" and survive the rural poverty she was facing alone in a hostile environment. Grandma left the soil behind to go to the city, and with only a third grade education, she pushed her family socially forward, so that they became professionals and achieved middle class status. But this achievement came at the price of two vital gifts: our creativity and our connection to Earth. Just as Grandma had burnt the poems that her soul expressed, one by one her children became "sensible" adults seeking to survive by making money and "staying afloat" —betraying their secret dreams and talents. Grandma's garden went from having trees and roses to a cement platform where her children store their cars.

I am the ambassador of poetry and creativity in my family. That's like being the majestic swan in a family of lovable, but ordinariness-worshipping ducklings —one gets to feel weird and becomes the *Ugly Duckling* until one discovers her true nature.

Creativity then became both my gift and my wound. This painful, glorious paradox trained me as a transformation artist. Like a healer, the transformation artist masters the art of transmuting the lead of dissonance, pain and heartbreak into the gold of harmony, power and love.

My poetry, my stories and my live journeys are ceremonies that bring you back to the source of your power: your radiant soul.

I confess: I am an eavesdropper.

I hear people's dreams, their complaints, their fears and their struggles. I hear people talking in the subway, on their cell phones, at my events, during my consultations and teachings, as my friends or in social media and online forums.

In the stories they tell people often focus on their problems, limitations, diseases and lack. In my stories I give them back their own stories —transmuted into possibilities, revelations, transformation and creative potential. When they hear these stories and poems they recognize themselves. That opens a space for them to see themselves in a different light; as the protagonists of their life, as creators of their world.

So yes, I am a storyteller. But more than that: I am a story alchemist. I use story, poetry and art to help you change your story of playing small and hiding in plain sight to the story of you living your brilliance right now.

I've discovered that all that we truly are, have and love travels with us in our very *Presence*. I can often see people's talents, soul's brilliance and life purpose in their *Energy Field*.

You may find this hard to believe, but sometimes a person's *DreamSelf*, her *Inner Children* or *Spiritual, Creative Selves* jump out of their Energy Field and wave at me.

"Here, here!" They call out to me. "We know you can see us. Hear my voice! I'm a great singer. Look at me! I'm an artist. Feel my strong intent. I'm a leader. Touch my hands. I'm a healer. Could you help our Self trust these gifts? We need to express this and she's got us locked up!"

Sometimes I even interview people, as I have been doing for **"De Pueblo en Pecho,"** *(A Heartful of my People)* —an ongoing poetry collection about the Puerto Ricans who migrated to the USA. Some of these poems were featured, together with the interviews, in *Viva Magazine/Daily News*. I also presented them on stage at *Teatro La Tea*, New York in 1990 as the poetry performance **Mujericana** (*Womerican*).

I have taken my poetry to the stage for decades, including poetry performances such as "Arte*es*Ana" and "Sister, Love Thyself," spoken word presentations such as "Bewomaning Verses" "El eterno soldado" and "El duende en los ojos" and ceremonial poems such as "Venus Altar," The Stolen Light," Follow the Pain," "Your Reasons to Fight," "The Churning" "The Mirror Lies/El espejo miente" and "Butterfly Woman Journey," among others.

My poetry has also been featured in the bilingual anthology **Abriendo Camino** *(Breaking Ground: Anthology of Puerto Rican Women Writers in New York 1980-2012)*, edited by Dr. Myrna Nieves and published by Editorial Campana with the support of Boricua College.

My poetry is a Rites of Passage from pain to love, an alchemy to transform your wounds into your power, a ceremony of soulful transformation and a journey from ordinary you to magical, extraordinary you.

I am also a shaman. As a modern, non-religious, non-denominational shaman I help you create magic in your life. But magic is not a parlor trick or childish ignorance.

Magic is a shift of perception that changes how you see your situation, changing how you respond to your circumstances and therefore changing the world you create through that response.

I work with imagination, energy and perception. It's a generational progression. You see, my grandpa was an electrician. My father was an engineer. I am the next level. I work with pure energy, with quantum miracles.

My poems, stories and events raise consciousness about the causes that I am passionate about:

- **Women's empowerment through the arts**
- **Women's self-esteem and Feminine Leadership**: The *Sacred Feminine* and the gifts of the *Sacred Feminine* in women
- **Heart-based change**: The *Alchemical Power of the Heart* and the qualities of the heart for coherent living, transformation and change-making.
- **Diversity and change-making**: Diversity, freedom and democracy and how we create them in our personal life through *Creative Freedom Alchemy*™ without creating a reactive, fear-based resistance and struggle MO.
- **Law of Attraction, manifestation**: Employing your creativity to manifest your dreams
- **Personal Transformation** through *Creative Freedom Alchemy*™, *Story Alchemy*™ and *Artchemy*™
- **The Art of Self-healing:** Transmuting the lead of problems, crisis, disease and loss into the gold of solutions, transformation, harmony and love.
- **Earth consciousness** and reconnecting to the Natural and Sacred World and
- **Creativity.** Awakening your Creative Genius. Reclaiming your vast creative potential. Freeing your imagination, unfolding your potential and living your brilliance. Employing your creativity to create the life you want. Creativity as the first trait for success in the 21st century.

As a poet, I am also a healer.

I heal the broken strands in the *Weave of Self*—in your Energy Field—through the poetry I channel combined with my voice, intention, images and music. These vibrations transform the emotional environment and help audiences to process stagnant emotions that —if unattended— may solidify into disease. Releasing stress, emptying the mind, uplifting your vibration, transmuting emotions, connecting to your *Sacred Self*, your divinity and embracing harmony are gifts I bring with my poetry and ceremonial poems.

In these events audiences are renewed and reconnected with life, earth and with the deepest truth and gifts within themselves.

This is what I do in **"The Tao of Trees,"** which is also available as a live poetry journey. If you lead an organization or event and would like these poems as an event or if you'd like a ceremonial poem to open or close your special event, visit this page and I'll call you back: **http://dreamalchemist.com/tao-presenters.**

If you are a creative person —especially a creative woman— and you want to open your wings and employ your creativity to live your brilliance, I invite you to join my *Brilliance Tribe* to receive new poems, flash stories, discounts and invitations to my live shamanic journeys.

Get my Brilliance Manifesto at: **http://mariamar.com/manifesto**

If you enjoy fantasy, magical stories and women's fiction, then get **a free anthology of shamanic stories with shamanic insights** by visiting this page: **http://dreamalchemist.com/join/**

I'll leave you with this thought:

Spirit, Earth Mother and her creatures and all the Universal Forces are your Creation Partners. They are listening. They will answer your questions. They will bring you solutions, allies and resources if you tune into your soul and call out from there. Poetry is not a literary genre that writers invented. Poetry —and more exactly the Living Metaphor— is the language of the soul, the language of the body, the language of life and the very language of the universe. I invite you to these poems as a door that opens for you a new way of communicating with the Universe, starting with listening to your Soul and connecting with Trees.

Where is Maria Mar?

Main Contact at:

Watch the Dream Alchemist TV Show and contact me at:
http://dreamalchemist.com

Book a 30-minute Courtesy Conversation to see how I can help you at:
http://www.vcita.com/v/mariamar

Email me at: **shamansdancepublishing@gmail.com**

Browse through my stores

General Store
http://dreamalchemist.com/store
Books only
http://dreamalchemist.com/storetag/books/
Tao of Trees Store
https://gumroad.com/taotrees

My online publications

Blog
Live your Brilliance
Enjoy great articles, videos, stories, poetry and inspiration.
http://www.mariamar.com

The Bewomaning Magazine
Be the Goddess dancing inside you
http://bewomaning.com

Catch the Dream Express
Feminine shamanic insights to manifest your dreams
http://catchthedreamexpress.com

Social Media

Facebook:
http://www.facebook.com/DreamAlchemist
Twitter:
http://twitter.com/DreamAlchemist
LinkedIn
http://www.linkedin.com/in/catchthedreamexpress
Pinterest
http://pinterest.com/dreamalchemist/

Communities/Memberships

Join my **Story Lovers Club** to get VIP Notices for my new or discounted *Story Journeys* and co-create new stories with me at:
https://storyloversclub.zenler.com/

Join my Brilliance Tribe
Join the Brilliance Tribe of creative women living their brilliance:
http://dreamalchemist.com/join

The Artchemist Journey
Awaken your Magical Creative Genius and become your dream now
Take the first step in your journey to manifest: Align with your Dream. It's free! No credit card. No pre-payment. No obligation. You'll get VIP Notice when the next Artchemist Journey opens.
https://catchthedreamexpress.zenler.com/free

Request Maria Mar for your Events

Speaker Maria Mar: Find out more about Maria Mar as a speaker and check out the storytelling, performance, ceremonial and transformational presentations available for your site at **http://dreamalchemist.com/speaker-maria-mar/**

Are you interested in presenting Maria Mar at your event? For **The Tao of Trees** events, go to: **http://dreamalchemist.com/tao-presenters**. For other events, go to: **http://dreamalchemist.com/presentation-request.**

Other Books by Maria Mar

FICTION

Angelina and the Law of Attraction

Shamanic Fantasy novel

Angelina is at the edge of giving up on her talents to follow an average formula for success. Just then her desperate soul summons a magical being who detours the train. Will Angelina trust this guide and save her dream? Or will she continue to her planned destination, missing her great destiny?

Angelina and the Law of Attraction *(A Woman's Ride from her Pressing Problems to her Brightest Potential)"* is a shamanic fantasy that takes you into a magical journey of manifestation using little known *Sacred Feminine* shamanic secrets of the Law of Attraction. Sit besides Angelina in the Dream Express as the whimsical Dragonfly Diva guides her through overwhelming fears, seemingly insurmountable obstacles and challenge after challenge while Angelina employs her creativity to manifest her dream. *Available in print or digital formats.* Read more at:
http://dreamalchemist.com/store/angelina-the-law-of-attraction/

A Place for Roses

Shamanic Fantasy Novella (with optional workbook)
Have you opened a space in your life for what you want? Join me in one of my own transformational journeys as I discover that it is not enough to want, not even to work hard to get or create what we want. We need to open a space inside us to receive it. This is a real-life story told from a shamanic perspective.

This inspirational story is a first-person narrative of me as I addressed my issues with wealth, health and love and discovered that they were part of my *Family Karma* —all during a bitter-sweet family holiday. **http://dreamalchemist.com/store/a-place-for-roses/**

Bewomaning Tales Series

The **Bewomaning Experience™** is a Rite of Passage for the 21st Century Woman. The blueprint for these rites is transmitted through stories. In the **Bewomaning Tales Series** Maria Mar shares each of the feminine actualization stages she experienced in her training as a *Woman of Power* through stories that she wrote during her healing process. These stirring stories are written in a language that will make your female soul sit up and sing. The stories take the shape of long stories, novellas or novels and are embedded with insights from the *Sacred Feminine School of Wisdom*.

Available now in digital format (PDF):

- **The Embrace: The Power of Zero**: A woman discovers that Zero is not only a place of loss. It is a place of possibility. *(Shamanic fantasy novella)* at: **https://gumroad.com/l/theembrace**

- **Awakening the Rose**: A Woman dives into her loss to grow her love *(Shamanic romance novella)* at: **https://gumroad.com/l/alchemicalrose**

Storybooks

My storybooks are delightful shamanic stories —often full of humor and wonder, as well as shamanic insights— that you can use as blueprints to experience deep transformation. You can also get the *Story Alchemy* for these stories in the form of multi-media playsets that provide a fun, creative life-laboratory around the story so that you can apply it to your life and achieve the transformation you want.

- **Little Deer and the Sacred Heart:** A moving story of how a troubled girl discovered the power of her heart. If the *Path of Beauty* or *the Path of the Heart* called to you, you will love this story!

    Get the storybook in any digital format for your device at: **https://gumroad.com/l/littledoe**

Get the playset with the storybook, audio laboratory and playbook at:
https://gumroad.com/l/growlovelivejoy

- **Joy and the Goldfish:** A creative woman who feels that the colors of her life are fading finds out that she has a *Human Creative Palette* she can use to magically paint her life with the colors of her *True Self*. If the *Paths of Co-creation, Transformation* or *Freedom* called you, then check this story out.

Get the storybook in any digital format for your device at:
https://gumroad.com/l/joyandgoldfish

Get the playset with the storybook, audio laboratory and playbook at:
https://gumroad.com/l/playset-masterlife

- **The Pregnant Woman who Forgot her Belly:** *A LifeBite story*. The LifeBite Stories are bite-size stories based on a real incident that I witness or experience in the Big Apple. In this *LifeBite* story, a pregnant woman is crossing the street with the red light against her when she drops a paper. Forgetting her belly, she bends to catch it just as a car drives towards her. Includes the story, shamanic insights and a ceremony to birth your *DreamBaby*. If the *Path of Transformation* called you find out more at: **https://gumroad.com/l/pregnantlady**

Pachamama Collection

The Pachamama Collection gathers my stories about Earth Mother, trees and the Natural and Sacred World.

Song of the Ocean is a humorous fantasy tale great to read as a family. Along with mermaids and a heroic lobster, there's education about global warming and how it affects our oceans while also throwing some shiny insight into the creative use of emotions. For kids of all ages. Grandmas have loved reading this with their girls. Read more at: **https://gumroad.com/l/songofocean**

Enjoy my Story Journeys

I create stories that are journeys for your transformation, healing, manifestation and liberation. *Story Journeys* are a way to achieve change through the medium of *Story Alchemy*™ and *Artchemy*™ —as each story includes modules with:

- **Shamanic insights, teachings and tools** to create the life you want and address specific problems you may be facing.
- **Ceremonies that you can use to quicken your transformation.**
- **Story Alchemy™ experiences** that allow you to use the story as a blueprint for your life, including journal writing questions and conscious living practices.
- **Artchemy™ —arts and crafts and other creative activities** as alchemy to create the change you want.
- **Bonus materials** in the form of Artspirations, poems, poetry journeys, special reports and more
- **Resources** such as books, links, materials and support services.

Try this magical stories treasure chest for Free!

Register for the free trial here:
https://storyloversclub.zenler.com/trial

NON-FICTION

From Hiding in Plain Sight to Living my Brilliance

A Journey to Unlock your Creativity, Share your Gifts and Embody your Purpose
Personal Growth for Creative Women with a playbook and bonus 41-day Story Journey

This book reveals my personal story from:
- Doubting my creativity
- Holding back because of feeling insufficient
- Believing I could not have the talents I longed for, and
- Living a double life, doing a job to pay the bills and paying to do my art "on the side"...

TO

- Freeing my Creative Genius
- Making a living from my art the minute I made an oath, and
- Embodying my purpose in a business, dozens of books and products and a brilliant life.

ALSO:

- Find why Creatives have so much self-doubt and find it hard to believe they can make a living from their gifts and why this is their time.
- Discover why you as a woman may hate the words "success, power and leadership," how that is affecting you and a new definition of power.

In the book I've included a playbook for you to use your creativity to change your *Tiny Story* and begin to live your brilliance. For the price of one meal you can get the book and playbook, around a dozen visual aids and posters plus a 41 day *Story Journey* to inspire, motivate and direct you to **Wake Up your Creative Genius** now.

- Get the digital format now at: **https://gumroad.com/l/mybrilliance**
- The paperback edition comes out in Fall 2018. Pre-order the paperback here: **https://gumroad.com/l/brilliance-paperback**

Rewrite your Fairy Tales for Success: Unleash your Greatness

Personal growth for women
Discover how your favorite childhood fairy tales reveal the secret "curse" or prohibition that you suffered as a child and that is still enchanting you out of your greatness.

Rewrite your Fairy Tales for Success *(Unleash your Greatness)* is a book especially written for spiritual, creative women. It presents six archetypal mother-daughter wounds and shows you how they became a "curse" that sabotages your current success and happiness.

This book then uses six popular fairy tales to help you transmute those "curses" or wounds into *Feminine Leadership,* leading to your authentic, out-of-the-box success. Go to: **https://gum.co/fairytales**

Give Yourself Permission to Deserve Success

Success Journey for Creative Women
Book 1 in The Successful Creative Woman Series

Women are struggling to achieve success or fulfillment but find themselves in a painful inner war that does not allow them to create, receive, enjoy or even **feel** their success. Brilliant female leaders confess that they do not **feel** like a success in spite of intellectually knowing what they contribute to the community. Thousands of women diminish their gifts while they overwork and still feel inadequate. Women are all but absent from the big stages of the world. What is going on? Discover the seven *Emotional Prohibitions* that women inherit from our herstory and family and that are still active in the 21st culture.

This book is a portal for spiritual creative women to address the first **Emotional Prohibition** and give themselves the first *Emotional permission:* to DESERVE success, fulfillment and happiness. **https://gum.co/deserve-success**

For **The Successful Creative Woman Journey**, see the **Coming Soon Section.**

COMING SOON!

Here's my line up of books for 2018-2023. To receive VIP notices when my books come out, as well as my monthly Love Letter, Dream Alchemist TV Show preview and other treats, join my *Brilliance Tribe* here: http://dreamalchemist.com/join/

Spring 2019

Mary Magdalene and the Alchemical Rose:

Mystery Teachings on the Power of your Heart from the Sacred Feminine School of Wisdom
Mary Magdalene offers heart-opening insights and life-changing spiritual transmissions about the power, alchemy and wisdom of your heart and how the qualities of your heart are also your *Feminine Gifts*. She reveals how reclaiming your heart's wisdom and expressing your *Feminine Gifts* is the path to healing humanity in the 21st Century and helps you to awaken the Goddess within.

Fall 2019

The Successful Creative Woman Journey

Are you a creative woman —a writer, artist, healer or a woman with a spiritual message… BUT you are not sharing your gifts, wisdom or message with the world. What holds you back? Discover and break through the *Emotional Prohibitions* to success that women secretly inherit. This book series supports you in achieving creative success. Books are dripped one chapter a week, with journaling questions, *Conscious Living Practices,* resources and *Artchemy™ Projects* that empower you to give yourself the *Emotional Permissions* for success, fulfillment and happiness.

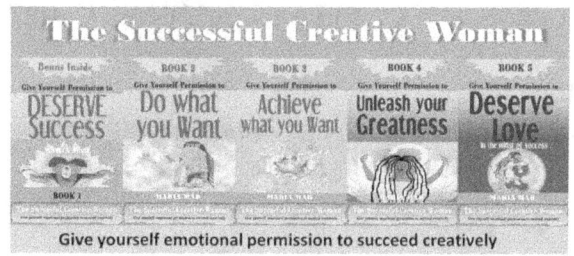

FALL 2020

Bewomaning Tales Series
The Bewomaning Experience ™ is a ceremonial experience of transformation through story and art as alchemy for your female actualization.

The Bewomaning Tales & Journeys are the series of stories I wrote as I was healing my own emotional wounds and being trained as a *Woman of Power*. Each story shares how I walk a stage in the female actualization path.

The series includes about a dozen books with shamanic stories; each story weaving a healing path that provides *Rites of Passage for the 21st Century Woman*. Wrap this story quilt around your heart and heal the shaming, prohibitions, guilt, self-neglect and other emotional wounds that break your woman's heart.

These stirring stories are written in a language that will make your female soul sit up and sing. The stories take the shape of long stories, novellas or novels and are embedded with insights from the *Sacred Feminine School of Wisdom*.

These stories deal with issues I have faced and that women face every day, including sexual shaming and relationship addictions, *Inner Wars* between love and power, spirituality and activism and other key values, self-sabotage, *Inner Divorce* between the *Sacred Masculine* and the *Sacred Feminine,* issues with self-value, wealth and love, the struggle to serve others while living your purpose, and other women's issues.

I am editing these stories and preparing supporting experiences for them and **The Bewomaning Tales & Journeys** will launch on Fall 2020.

SPRING 2021

Bewomaning Verses

Shed your Identity Rags and Don your Goddess Gown
A poetic Rites of Passage for the 21st Century Woman

The Book

Accompany poet-shaman Maria Mar as she shares more than three decades of poems nourishing her transformation into a *Woman of Power*. In these poems Maria used creative writing to transmute childhood and adolescent wounds into *Personal Medicine* as well as to shed the *Identity Rags* that kept her as a woman from valuing and sharing her unique gifts and blossoming in her full potential —on her own terms. These poems will awaken memories of your childhood, your dreams, your gifts and your wounds so that you can heal your

female wounds and awaken the Goddess in you. They will move you from learned limitations to your delightful potential.

This poetry book will include a Feminine Actualization Journal Writing and a Poetry Writing Edition.

FALL 2021

From Reactive to Proactive Change-making

Creative Freedom Alchemy

Memories of a Baby-boomer Feminist, Artist and Change-maker

What if instead of fighting, resisting and reacting we proactively created the world we want? Through stories of her life as a feminist, activist, artist and change-maker Maria Mar calls women, people of color and all change-makers to become the change we want in the world through a love-based proactive process she calls *Creative Freedom Alchemy*.

To receive VIP notices when my books come out, as well as my monthly love letter, Dream Alchemist TV Show preview and other treats, join my *Brilliance Tribe* here:
http://dreamalchemist.com/join/

Spring 2022

Inlak'esh

You are my Other Self
Diving into our Loss to Find our Love
Sacred Poetry

Those of us who seek beauty, healing and to create a life of love and integrity and a world of freedom and justice often face the pain of cruelty, injustice, abuse and oppression with a sense of despair, failure or struggle. In this book poet, change-maker and shaman Maria Mar dives into human pain, heart-breaking abuse and even evil to find the brilliant jewel of love, compassion and Oneness that can strengthen our capacity to create a better life and a better love.

Fall 2023

Through the Wound on Earth Runs the Song of the Waters
Three generations of women struggle to free their creative potential
(Shamanic Novel)

This is the novel I promised my grandmother many decades ago, before she lost her memories, her hope and her life.

It is the fictional story of three generations of women facing a harsh world and how their pain ran like blood until it rose as a song of joy, creativity and liberation.

Tender encounters with my grandmother mix with traumatic family clashes and are woven with the magic fiber of shamanic ceremonies to reweave pain into power and loss into love.

To receive VIP notices when my books come out, as well as my monthly love letter, Dream Alchemist TV Show preview and other treats, join my *Brilliance Tribe* here:
http://dreamalchemist.com/join/

More Poetry!

Maria's poetry featured in this anthology

Breaking Ground Anthology

Anthology of Puerto Rican Women Writers in New York 1980-2012.
Edited by Dr. Myrna Nieves.
Published by Editorial Campana

I am so honored, my beautiful friends! My poetry was included in the **Breaking Ground** Poetry Anthology, edited by my dear friend and well-known author and cultural leader Myrna Nieves and published by Campana Publishers.

This important bilingual anthology ~ten years in the making~ gathers the work of Puerto Rican women poets and narrators living in New York who have been writing, inspiring, empowering and educating our communities from 1980 to 2012.

- Do you want to know the faces and voices that have sustained, inspired, educated and empowered New York Latinos for more than a decade?
- Would you like to hear the often marginalized voices of Puerto Rican women poets and writers?
- Would you like to enrich your family's cultural wellbeing with beautiful poems about our current, modern reality?
- Do you love poetry? Spoken-word? Cultural events?
- Do you want poems about love, family, abuse, belonging, loneliness, liberation, our people, life, death, the experience of women and Latinas, bilingualism, racial issues, self-love and cultural pride? Grab this groundbreaking book!
- Are you empowering your young children or students by nurturing their bilingual pride or generating consciousness about diversity?

Then this important anthology is a must-have in your home or classroom library. It's available at Amazon here: **https://www.amazon.com/Breaking-Ground-Anthology-escritoras-puertorriquenas/dp/1934370169**

Poems are written in Spanish or English. When you purchase the book, email me to get the translation of my poems and my digital autograph!

Tree Love Pledge

Check the items below that you want to pledge yourself to do. Print and place in your fridge. Read out loud once a day for 90 days, to imprint the pledge in your habits.

- I, _____(*Your name*) pledge to connect lovingly to trees and give back to them in gratitude for all they do for me.

- **I will do this internally** by sending love to the trees in my area and in the endangered zones and the rainforests of the world. I will spend about a minute a day consciously breathing into my heart and sending love to the trees with my exhalation (carbon dioxide).

- **I will do this locally** by helping plant and maintain trees in my community, hugging the trees around me, meditating, singing or communing with them.

- I will join a tree-planting or saving organization in my area.

- **Other:** I will do this: *(Name what you want to do locally. Make sure it feels good so that you stick with it and do it with love).*

- **I will do this globally** by reducing my use of paper, buying recycled paper or packaging and/or recycling paper, boxes and other packaging and by reducing or eliminating those activities that threaten the lives of trees. *(See Resource Section)*

- **I will do this creatively** through creative activities recycling paper products with my students/members/children using cardboard boxes like cereal, cracker and other packages for creative projects,

- By buying art that recycles paper products.

- I will do this with Maria Mar and the Poet-trees by joining the **Street Team** for the **Tree Love Campaigns**. (Sign up here: http://dreamalchemist.com/tao-street-team)

I _____ make this pledge today _____ .

www.ingramcontent.com/pod-product-compliance
Lightning Source LLC
Chambersburg PA
CBHW080343170426
43194CB00014B/2663